Contents

PART ONE THE NORMANS IN ENGLAND

1.1	Who were the Normans?	
1.2	The Norman World	6
1.3	England before the Normans	8
1.4	Who wants to be King?	10
1.5	1066: The Battle of Hastings	12
1.6	The Death of Harold	14
1.7	The Normans conquer England	16
1.8	The Bayeux Tapestry	18

PART TWO IRELAND, WALES AND SCOTLAND

2.1	Ireland before the Normans	20
2.2	Dermot of the Foreigners	22
2.3	The Coming of Strongbow	24
2.4	Henry II comes to Ireland	26
2.5	**CASE STUDY:** John de Courcy and Ulster	28
2.6	Wales and the Normans	32
2.7	Scotland and the Normans	33

PART THREE LIFE IN THE MIDDLE AGES

3.1	The Feudal System	34
3.2	Castles 1: Motte and Bailey	36
3.3	Castles 2: Monuments in Stone	38
3.4	Castles 3: Life in a Castle	40
3.5	Medieval Warfare	42
3.6	The Medieval Village	44
3.7	The Medieval Town	48
3.8	The Church	52
3.9	The Monastery	54
3.10	1348 The Black Death	58
3.11	1381 The Peasants' Revolt	60
3.12	The Norman Legacy	62

INFORMATION BANK

KINGS OF ENGLAND	63
CHRONOLOGY	63
Index	64

1.1 Who were the Normans?

Part of the Bayeux Tapestry showing William feasting. You can learn about the Bayeux Tapestry on page 18

The Bayeux Tapestry - 11th century. By special permission of the City of Bayeux.

Introduction

Welcome to the Middle Ages!

But what are they?

When someone is not very young and still not grey and wrinkled, they are called **middle-aged**. It's a bit like that with history. The term **Middle Ages** means simply the bit that comes between **Ancient History** (Julius Caesar, pyramids, etc.) and **Modern History** (Henry VII, Hitler, Margaret Thatcher, etc.) This book is about the second half of the Middle Ages — from about 1066 to 1485. By this stage, you should already have learned something about the **early** Middle Ages (St. Patrick, St. Columba, Saxons, Vikings, etc.) We are going to start with the **Normans** who came to England in 1066 and to Ireland in 1169.

> **B**
>
> *These* [Normans] *certainly cultivated a sense of identity and common characteristics which ... tended to be of a military and political type. Ferocity, boundless energy, cunning, and a capacity for leadership were their heritage, to which modern scholars would add supreme adaptability and a simple piety.*

D. Nicolle and A. McBride
The Normans, 1987

The Normans

So who were they?

The word "Norman" means Northman or man from the north. Today, some people, like the author of this book, are called Norman. Tradition has it that the Normans were descended from Viking pirates who settled in northern France in the ninth century. In 911 Charles III, King of France, came to terms with them by granting Rollo (the Norman leader) the right to rule upper Normandy, probably in return for the Normans becoming Christian and giving Charles III military help.

However, not everyone who lived in Normandy was Viking so, by 1066, the Normans had intermarried with the local population and were as much French as Viking.

What were the Normans like?

We can learn something of what the Normans were like by looking at what modern historians say about them, and at the comments made about them by writers at the time.

Read Sources B - D and see what you think.

C

In 1066 the Normans, as they are now, were very fussy about their clothes and enjoyed their food, but they were not greedy. They are so used to war that they can hardly live without it.

William of Malmesbury *Deeds of the Kings of the English* 1125

Traditions are ideas and stories that come from so long ago no-one knows who first thought of them or if they are actually true.

Piety means holiness.

D

The Frankish bishops said, 'Anyone who received such a gift ought to bend down and kiss the King's foot.' But Rollo said, 'Never will I bend my knees to anyone, nor will I kiss anyone's foot.' But the Franks insisted, so Rollo ordered a certain soldier to kiss the King's foot. The soldier immediately took hold of the King's foot, lifted it up to his mouth and kissed it without kneeling down, so that the King was toppled over backwards.

Dudo, *The Manners and Deeds of the First Dukes of Normandy*, written about 1020.

?

1. In which period of history would you place each of the following: Hitler; Julius Caesar; Rollo; 1066; 100 BC; 1690? (see page 4)

2. Using Sources B and C make a list of words and phrases used to describe the Normans.

3. What does Source D tell us about the attitude of Rollo and his soldiers?

1.2 The Norman World

By 1000 the Normans were firmly established in Normandy and in the century which followed, the Normans began to expand their military power into other parts of France, into the British Isles and, as the maps show, even further afield. Until they conquered England in 1066, the Norman leaders were only dukes and in Normandy itself they continued to be dukes. **William the Conqueror** was both **King William I** of England and **Duke William of Normandy**.

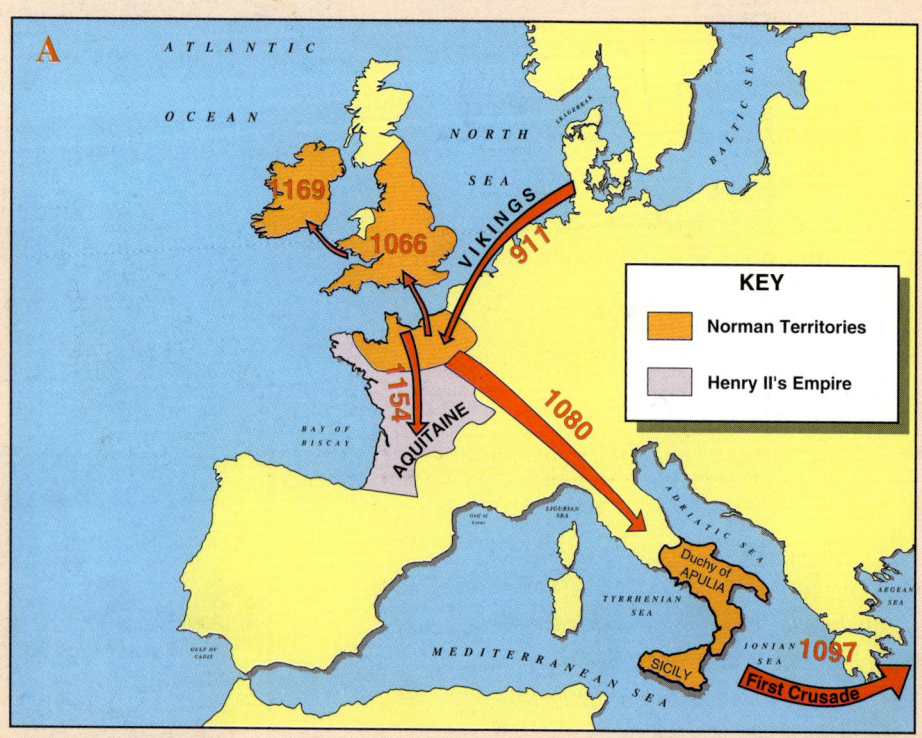

Western Europe in 1200 showing the areas ruled by the Normans.

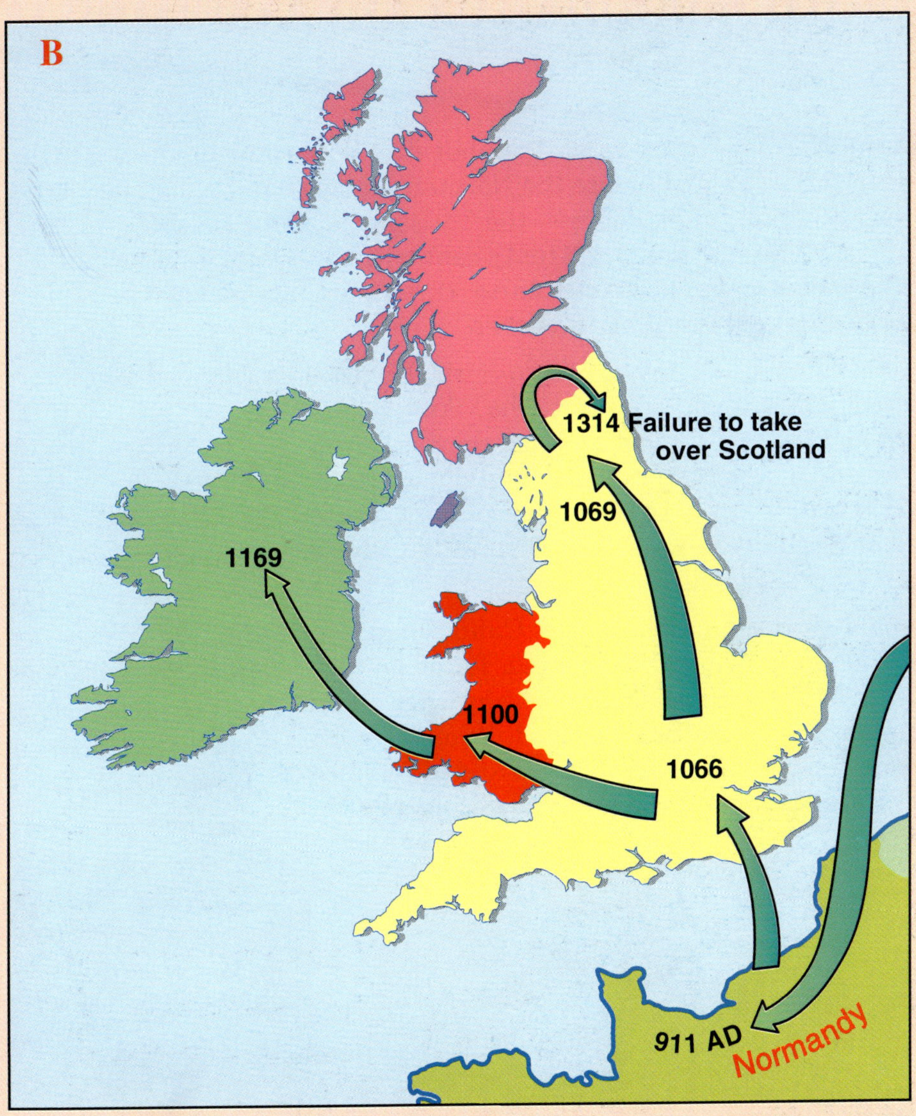

B

Norman expansion in the British Isles, also showing Normandy.

Activities

1 Trace the maps and put coloured versions of them in your own book.

2 Using the maps, construct a timeline from 911 to 1311 showing the main events in the Norman expansion in the British Isles, e.g. 1169 Normans arrive in Ireland.

1 In what order did the Normans conquer the following places: England, Ireland, Normandy, Sicily, Wales?

1.3 England before the Normans

Most books on the Normans start with 1066, but it is important to know a little bit about England as it was in the years just before the Normans came. The English people before 1066 were a blend of several groups of invaders — the Celts (up to about 100 BC), the Anglo-Saxons (about 450-650) and the Vikings (ninth and tenth centuries). England is named after the Angles (Anglo-Saxons) whose land was called **Angleland**. If you say that quickly it becomes **England**. The French name for England is still **Angleterre**.

Before the Vikings came in 793 AD, the Anglo-Saxon England was divided into several smaller kingdoms, e.g. Northumbria, Mercia, Wessex. The Viking threat unified the Saxons and the first king of all England was Alfred the Great (849-900) and his successors ruled England until the Danes conquered the country in 1014. The Danes made Canute (1016-1035) King of England as well as of Denmark. Canute was a very famous king. (See Source A).

To secure his hold on the English throne, Canute married Emma, the widow of the previous Saxon king. Later he also became King of Norway, so when he died in 1035 he ruled three kingdoms — Denmark, Norway and England. When Canute died his various sons fell out among themselves and his empire was divided. The English took the opportunity to restore a Saxon king.

A

Canute, it was said, was once addressed as "Lord and Master of the sea as well as of the land". He thereupon conveyed his chair to the shore when the tide was rising, and forbade the waves to come nearer. When they had splashed over his feet he turned and rebuked his courtiers, saying that God alone ruled heaven, earth and sea.

Story of the British Nations ed. Walter Hutchinson 1939

B
The Last Kings of Saxon England

- ✖ 978-1014 Ethelred II (the Unready)
- ➤ 1014-1016 Sweyn
- ➤ 1016-1035 Canute
- ➤ 1035-1040 Harold I (Harefoot)
- ➤ 1040-1042 Hardicanute
- ✖ 1042-1066 Edward the Confessor
- ✖ 1066 Harold II (Godwin)

  ➤ Danish
  ✖ Saxon

Edward the Confessor 1042 - 1066

Edward was the son of the last Saxon king, Ethelred II. He had lived in exile in Normandy from boyhood to middle age. His mother, Emma, had been Norman, and by the time Edward came to England as king he spoke French, loved things Norman and dressed like a Norman. He was also very religious (thus his nickname **The Confessor**). He had been reared by Norman monks and spent a lot of his time building new churches, like Westminster Abbey. Although he married a Saxon — his queen was the daughter of Earl Godwin and sister of the later King Harold — he remained a **celibate**. This means he had no sexual relations with his wife and so had no sons to succeed him when he died in 1066.

How the comet appears on the Bayeux Tapestry. The Latin translates as 'Here is the wondrous star'.

(The Bayeux Tapestry - 11th century. By special permission of the City of Bayeux.)

D

It happened that all through England such a sign in the heavens was seen as no man has seen before. Some men said that it was the star 'Comet', that some men call the long-haired star. It appeared first on the eve of April 14th, and so shone all seven nights.

Anglo-Saxon Chronicle 1066

Edward's Death

Edward the Confessor died in January 1066. Harold Godwin was almost immediately crowned king. This angered William of Normandy who claimed that Edward had promised him the throne.

Then in April a strange sign appeared in the sky (Sources C and D). We now know that this 'star' was **Halley's comet** which appears roughly every 76 years. It last appeared in 1986. If you missed it then — tough! It won't be back until 2061. In 1066 no one knew what a comet was, so they thought that it must be a sign from God that terrible things were going to happen.

To rebuke some one means to scold or tell them off.

A **tapestry** is a piece of cloth, often very large, which has a design or picture woven into it with coloured threads.

Activities

1. You are an English monk in 1066. Describe the appearance of the comet and explain what it might mean.
2. Use your library to find out about (a) Ethelred the Unready (b) Canute (c) Edward the Confessor.

1. Compare Sources C and D. What can we learn from Source C that Source D does *not* tell us?
2. What can we learn from Source D that Source C does *not* tell us?
3. What single thing do *both* sources tell us?

1.4 Who wants to be King?

Harold had become king, but two other people also thought they should rule England. These were the King of Norway and the Duke of Normandy. A third alternative was Edgar the Atheling.

King of Norway

Name: **Harald** Hardrada (Hard Raider)

Title: **Harald** III, King of Norway and Denmark (1047-66)

For: Claimed to be the true heir of Canute. Since Canute had ruled England as well as Norway and Denmark so should he. Harold Godwin's brother Tostig supported him and would supply an army and ships to help dethrone Harold.

Against: He was in Norway, not England. Most Englishmen preferred Harold. If he invaded England it would renew the old wars between Danes and English.

Prince Edgar

Name: Edgar the Atheling.

Title: Prince Edgar.

For: Great grandson of Ethelred the Unready. Grand nephew of Edward the Confessor. Thus a direct descendant of the Saxon royal family. Harold had only married into it.

Against: Only a boy so could not fight either Duke William of the King of Norway. Had been brought up in Hungary so had few supporters in England.

Harold

Name: Harold Godwin

Title: Harold II, King of England. Previously Earl of Wessex

For: Brother-in-law of Edward the Confessor. A good strong fighting leader. Very popular with most of the English. He had been *elected* king by the *Witan* (Saxon Council made up of bishops, nobles and advisers).

Against: William claimed that Harold had promised to support him as the next king, and had sworn to do so on holy relics.

William of Normandy

Name: William of Normandy.

Title: Duke of Normandy (since 1035).

For: Claimed that Edward the Confessor had promised him the throne of England. Claimed that Harold had sworn to back him as king. He was an experienced commander and had good equipment.

Against: Harold was already established as king. An invasion of England would require a fleet and could be very risky. He would have little support in England.

Harold's coronation. (The Bayeux Tapestry - 11th century. By special permission of the City of Bayeux.)

B

Harold was guilty of lying, cruelty and wickedness. In the three months he had been king many people had been badly treated. He had no right to be king.

Ordericus Vitalis *Ecclesiastical History of England and Normandy* 1135

C

As soon as Harold became king, he made it his job to stop unfair laws and make good ones. He was kind and polite to all men, but strictly punished all criminals. He ordered the arrest of all thieves and robbers. He worked very hard to defend his country, by land and at sea.

Florence of Worcester 1130 (Florence was a man!)

D

1065: yet did the wise king [Edward] entrust his kingdom to a man of high rank, to Harold himself, the noble earl who ever faithfully obeyed his noble lord [King Edward].

Anglo-Saxon Chronicle. Written in 1066

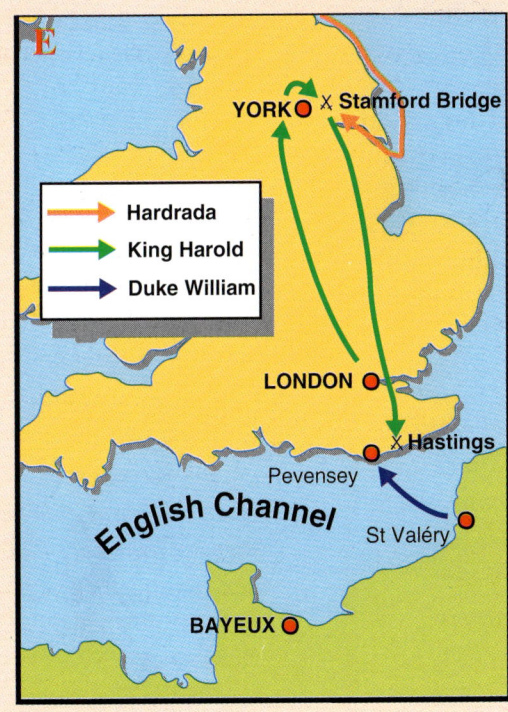

England, showing Harold's movements before the Battle of Hastings.

?

1. Read Sources B – D. In each case say whether they favour Harold or not. Explain your reasons.

2. Examine Source A. See if you can identify the objects Harold has been given to identify him as king — the sceptre (a long ornamented stick), the sword of state (representing justice), the crown, the orb (globe with a cross on top).

3. Suggest what the orb might represent.

Harold thought that William would attack first so he placed his army in the south of England at London. William did not come. Instead news came in September that Tostig and the King of Norway had landed in Yorkshire. Harold immediately marched north and fought a great battle at **Stamford Bridge** (25th September 1066). It was a total victory. Both Tostig and the King of Norway were killed. It took only a quarter of the Viking fleet to bring the survivors home.

Activities

1. Organise a debate in which speeches are made in support of Harold and William.
2. Write a letter from William to Odo his brother (Bishop of Bayeux) in June 1066, explaining why he was going to invade England.

1.5   1066: The Battle of Hastings

Shortly after his victory at Stamford Bridge, news reached Harold that William had landed in the south, at **Pevensey**. Harold immediately marched south, a distance of 400 kilometres, and arrived near **Hastings** on October 13. The next day William and Harold fought each other in battle. It was no easy victory, as the sources in this chapter show, but on the outcome rested the future of English history.

Battle of Hastings: a few facts

The Battle was not fought at Hastings at all, but at a place 10 kilometres away, now called **Battle**. Harold's men were drawn up a hill called Senlac. There were probably 5000-7000 men in each army. The battle began at 9.00 am and lasted until dusk, with no break for lunch or tea. Both Norman knights and English housecarls wore chain mail and the fashionable conical helmet with nose piece. Their shields were kite shaped, not round. Both armies had large numbers of half-armoured men with inferior weapons. The archers used short-bows, about 1.2 metres in length. (see Unit 3.5)

Pevensey Beach where William landed in 1066

A

B

Duke William, having intelligence of Harold's approach, ordered his troops to take to their arms on the morning of Saturday. He then heard mass, strengthening both body and soul by partaking of the consecrated host; he also reverently hung from his neck the holy relics on which Harold had sworn.

Ordericus Vitalis *Ecclesiastical History of England and Normandy* 1135

C

... braying [blowing] of trumpets announced the outset of battle on both sides. Eager and brave the Normans were first to attack ... The English hurled javelins and missiles of all sorts, dealing savage blows with their axes ... Then the knights rode forward ... they bravely engaged the enemy with their swords. The din of the shouting from the Normans on this side, from the barbarians [English] on that, could hardly be heard for the clash of their weapons and the groans of the dying.

William of Poitiers, chronicler to William, writing about 1071

D

The Norman infantry turned in flight ... almost the whole battle line of Duke William fell back, a fact which can be admitted without affront [insult] to the Normans ... The Normans imagined that their Duke had fallen, but he rushed after his retreating troops, dragged off his helmet and showed his bared head. 'Look at me!' he shouted, 'I am still alive! With God's help I shall win' ... They took new courage from his words and he himself rode on again at their head.

William of Poitiers.

To act **impetuously** means to act rashly, without a lot of thought.

A **holy relic** is part of a very holy person's body or belongings which is kept after his or her death as something which is very sacred.

- 12 -

E

William's knights charging at the Battle of Hastings.

F
The English who were so sure of themselves fought with all their might, they were so tightly massed that the men who were killed could hardly fall on the ground. The Normans realised that they could never overcome the vast army of their enemies ... They therefore withdrew, pretending to turn in flight. Some thousand or more of the English rushed boldly forward; suddenly the Normans turned their horses, cut off the force which was pursuing them, encircled them and massacred them to the last man. Twice the Normans used this trick with equal success.

William of Poitiers.

G
At last the English began to weary. Evening was now falling, they knew that their king with two of his brothers and many other great men had been killed. Those who remained were almost exhausted, and they realised that they could expect no more help.

They began to flee as swiftly as they could, some on foot, some along the roads, but most over the trackless country. The Normans eagerly carried on the pursuit, and striking the rebels in the back brought a happy end to this famous victory.

William of Poitiers.

H
The Normans had two military weapons which the English lacked, namely, archers and heavy armed cavalry. It was by the skilful and daring use of these that Duke William solved the difficult problem with which he was confronted, and at the end of a hard-fought day won the signal victory at Hastings, the most important in English History.

Sir John Edward Lloyd *Early History of the British Nations* 1939

I
That Hastings was a decisive defeat of infantry by cavalry-with-archers is, of course, a common place of History ... The fact was that Harold through his very energy in taking a large force to the north to deal with Hardrada, and then through his impetuosity in returning to meet William before he could deploy all the resources undoubtedly available to him, had greatly weakened his chances of success.

G W S Barrow
Feudal Britain 1956

> **?**
> 1. Make a list of possible reasons for William's victory in the Battle of Hastings.
> 2. Examine Sources A - I. Which are primary and which are secondary?
> 3. What points do Sources H and I agree about?

1.6 The Death of Harold

(The Bayeux Tapestry - 11th century. By special permission of the City of Bayeux.)

The Bayeux Tapestry shows the death of Harold. 'Harold Rex Interfectus Est'.

Activities

1. Use all the material on p 12-15 to write a description in your own words of the Battle of Hastings 1066. You might like to have the following parts:
   - William's landing at Pevensey
   - Harold's march south
   - Description of the fighting
   - Harold's death
   - William's victory

2. Use sources C, D, E to examine what happened to Harold's body. Construct a table like this.

	Source C	Source D	Source E
How was Harold killed? Who buried Harold? Where was he buried?			

Discuss the conclusion that can be made from this evidence.

Study all these sources to find out what happened to King Harold.

B

He fought bravely from nine in the morning until night time. He defended himself with such courage that the enemy thought they would never beat him. But sadly, as it started to get dark, Harold was wounded and killed.

Florence of Worcester, 1130

C

At last Harold fell after his brain had been split through by an arrow. But while the King was still breathing, one of the Normans ran up to him and cut off his leg. William had him beaten for this, and expelled him from the army.

He sent the body of King Harold to his mother. William did not want the large ransom that she had offered for the body. When she received it, she buried it at Waltham in the church which Harold himself had built.

Matthew of Westminster, writing about 1320.

D

He was wounded in many places, losing his left eye through an arrow which went into it. But, although beaten, he escaped to these parts. It is believed that he led the life of an anchorite, passing his days in one of the local churches, (until his death). The real identity of these two people was only revealed when they made their last confession.

Gerald of Wales, a monk, writing in 1188.

E

Harold had no badges on him and could not be identified by his face, only by certain marks on his body. King William gave it to William Malet for burial, and not to Harold's mother. She wanted to bury Harold herself and offered William her son's weight in gold. But the King thought that it was wrong to get money in this way. He did not think that Harold should be buried as his mother wanted, because so many men had died because of his greed. He said jokingly that, because Harold had tried so hard to guard the coast of England, he should be buried by the sea shore.

William of Poitiers writing about 1071

?

1. Examine Source A. Which figure do you think is Harold?
2. What do you think of the claims made by Gerald of Wales in Source D?

An anchorite is a hermit, someone who lives alone away from ordinary society.

1.7 The Normans conquer England

South-eastern England showing William's route from Hastings to London

William becomes King

The Battle of Hastings did not immediately make William King of England. William waited five days but no one came to offer him the crown. Then he marched along the coast to Dover and burnt the castle. This scared the people of Canterbury and when William neared their town they immediately surrendered.

Meanwhile in London all was confusion. Some wanted to fight on and make **Prince Edgar** King (see Unit 1.4). Others thought William should be offered the crown. William passed London along the south bank of the Thames, crossed the river at Wallingford and approached London from the west. At this time the city was on the north bank of the river. At Berkhamsted the chief earls and bishops, as well as Edgar, met him and accepted William as King. He was crowned on **Christmas Day 1066** at Westminster Abbey. William did not execute Prince Edgar. Edgar became involved in the northern rebellion (see below), but despite its failure, he outlived William and died in 1125.

Rebellion

However, although London had accepted William as King, not all of the country was pleased. In 1068 the people of **Exeter** refused to admit William to the city and a siege followed. William soon took the city and built a castle there. William instructed all his barons to build castles on the land he gave them. Most of these early castles were wooden. (See Unit 3.2)

In 1069 **Sweyn**, the new **King of Denmark** sent 300 ships to the north of England. William marched north but never managed to fight the Danes, who got into their ships and played cat and mouse with William for a week before sailing home.

In 1070 William took his revenge on the people of the north who had supported the Danes. He burnt their crops, destroyed their villages and probably caused a famine that killed thousands. This is known as the **Harrying of the North** (Source D).

> **B**
> *With God's help, the king easily conquered the city of Exeter when it rebelled. Part of the wall fell down accidentally and this made an opening for him. He attacked it very fiercely because one of the men standing on the wall had bared his bottom and broken wind in front of the Normans.*

A note of defiance! William of Malmesbury, writing about 1125

C

The fortifications called castles by the Normans were scarcely known in England and so the English — in spite of their courage and love of fighting — could put up only weak resistance to their enemies.

Orderic Vitalis *History of the Church* 1141

Local Hero — Hereward the Wake

One of the last places to resist William was the fenlands of Cambridgeshire. In 1071 this area consisted of miles of swamps and small islands. It was here that a colourful local character called Hereward the Wake used the Island of Ely as a base from which to raid Norman farms and villages. Many stories were told about him, most of them legend. His sword was called **Brainbiter**. In 1071 William sent an army to crush Hereward by building a causeway to the Isle of Ely. However, the causeway collapsed and many soldiers drowned.

It was rumoured that Hereward had used black magic to destroy the causeway. William built a tower and put a witch in it to cast a spell on Hereward, but Hereward's men burnt the tower and the witch. At last William found a secret route to the island and captured it. But Hereward the Wake escaped and it is not known where he went.

Right: The White Tower, Tower of London, built by William after the Conquest.

D

In the whole country there was famine. People were so hungry that they ate human flesh, as well as horses, dogs and cats. Some people became slaves to try and stay alive. Others left their country, but fell down in the middle of the journey and died.

It was horrific to see human corpses decaying in the houses and roads, and swarming with worms. There was a terrible smell, because no one was left to bury them, all having been killed by the sword or by the famine.

For nine years, no one lived in the villages between York and Durham. They became places where wild animals and robbers lurked, and they were a great danger to travellers.

Henry of Huntingdon, a monk, writing about 1120.

?

1. What, according to Source C was the value of castles?

2. How do you think the Saxons felt about castle building?

3. Why did the incident in Source B annoy William so much?

4. Does Source D approve or disapprove of what William did? Give reasons for your answer.

1.8   The Bayeux Tapestry

Harold, swearing on sacred relics, declares loyalty to William.
(The Bayeux Tapestry - 11th century. By special permission of the City of Bayeux.)

By far the best known source of information on the Norman conquest is the famous Bayeux Tapestry. The tapestry is a kind of cartoon strip picture story about William coming to England and fighting the Battle of Hastings in 1066. A proper tapestry has the picture actually woven into it, so the Bayeux Tapestry is technically an embroidery, not a tapestry.

Bayeux Tapestry
— It is 50cms high and 70 metres long.
— It is made of linen and embroidered in wool.
— It would stretch across the width of a football pitch.
— In the tapestry the Normans are called Franci (French)
— It shows 600 men, 200 horses, 50 dogs — and 3 women!
— Saxons are always shown with moustaches.
— Normans are shown with the back of their hair cut short.

The nave of Bayeux Cathedral, Normandy in 1990. Did the tapestry once decorate each side of it?

The tapestry is regarded as the Norman version of what happened in 1066, and the Anglo-Saxon Chronicles as the Saxon version. The tapestry uses over a third of its length (25 metres) to explain how Harold is sent to Normandy by Edward; how he is captured by a nasty chap called Count Guy of Ponthieu; how William rescues him, treats him well, goes campaigning with him and eventually Harold promises, on holy relics, to support William as King (Source A). In contrast, one of the Anglo-Saxon Chronicles mentions that Harold went to Normandy, but does not say what he went for.

Source D appears to show the Norman soldiers eating **kebabs** after they arrived in England. Since kebabs did not appear in England until the 14th century, some experts have claimed that either the tapestry is not as old as it was thought to be, or that it has been altered several times since it was made. Others argue that kebabs came to Europe via the Turks and that the Normans in Sicily had made contact with the Turks as early as 1040, so kebabs in 1077 are not impossible.

Activities

1 Using all the information in this section, write a short essay titled 'The Bayeux Tapestry'.

2 Copy some drawings from the tapestry into your notebook. Colour them and write a short comment on what each shows.

C

Above all it is to be remembered that it is a work in praise of Bishop Odo's part in the conquest ... He appears four times in the tapestry and every time he steals the scene.

Dr. J. B. McNulty, tapestry expert, U.S.A. 1992

The servants passing around lunch. Are these kebabs?

(The Bayeux Tapestry - 11th century. By special permission of the City of Bayeux.)

E

He became a bishop at the age of 20. He had no religious vocation. Youngest sons often went into the church. He had always dreamt of being a ... knight. On the tapestry you see him holding a club, not a sword. Priests couldn't spill blood. They could only batter their enemies to death.

Professor Francis Neveux, 1992, speaking about Odo

Is Odo coming to William's rescue?

Bishop Odo and the Tapestry

A recent writer, Dr. J.. B McNulty, has claimed that the tapestry gives Bishop Odo's version of events in 1066, not William's. Odo was William's half-brother. He was the Duke of Kent, as well as Bishop of Bayeux. He commissioned and paid for the tapestry, and it was probably made to hang at the consecration of Bayeux Cathedral in 1077. It is now accepted that he had it embroidered in England, probably Kent. The English were renowned experts in tapestry making.

1. Look at Source A. Some English experts claim that those who embroidered the tapestry have made Harold appear to be touching the relics reluctantly or with only a finger. What do you think?

2. Is Source B primary or secondary? Explain your reasons.

3. How does Source F support Source E?

4. Do you think the makers of the tapestry were better at showing people, animals or things? Answer with reference to the pictures on these pages.

- 19 -

2.1　Ireland before the Normans

A High Cross: The Cross of the Scriptures, Clonmacnoise Monastery, Co. Offaly.

It was to be a century after the Battle of Hastings before the Normans came to Ireland. Unlike England, the Anglo-Saxons had not settled in Ireland. Its population was a mixture of Celts and Vikings. Most Irish people spoke the Gaelic language and followed Gaelic laws. Trade was largely controlled by the five Viking ports. (see page 22, Source A)

Kings

Celtic society was very complicated. Ireland was divided into about eight main territories (page 22) each ruled by its own King. Each of these was divided further into sub-kingdoms each with its own ruler, who was subject to the main king. The most powerful of the eight kings was called the **High King**. The High King was rather like a champion boxer. He only remained High King as long as he was unbeaten. In 1166 the King of Tyrone, who was High King, was overthrown and killed in a rebellion by his sub-kings who then gave their support to **Rory O'Connor**, King of Connaught. O'Connor then became High King.

> B
> ... Be thou my soul's shelter, be thou my strong tower ...
> O raise thou me heavenward, great Power of my power High King of Heaven, thou heaven's bright sun...
> O grant me its joys after victory is won.

9th century Irish hymn, reflecting life at the time.

Activities

Divide your page into two columns. Title one **England** and the other **Ireland**. List the differences found in this unit.
E.g. England - one king.
　　　Ireland - several kings.

Religion

Ireland was famous for its Celtic monasteries. Compared to Norman monasteries their buildings were very simple, consisting of several small stone beehive shaped cells for the monks to live in, clustered around a small stone church. A wall for protection surrounded the whole settlement and a tall round tower was used to store holy treasures and protect monks if the Vikings attacked. Most monasteries had one of the famous high crosses. (Source A)

The Irish kings were generous patrons of the church. In 1134 Cormac McCarthy, King of Munster, built the lovely church on the Rock of Cashel, now called **Cormac's Chapel**. However, some English orders of monks had also set up abbeys in Ireland. The Cistercians (Unit 3.9) founded **Mellifont Abbey** in 1141.

C

They live on beasts ... while man usually progresses from the woods to the fields to towns ... this people despises agriculture ... Cultivated fields are indeed few in number through the neglect of the cultivators: nevertheless the land is naturally fertile and fruitful.

Gerald of Wales, 1189, describing the Irish.

The People

Unlike England, which had settled farming villages with people growing crops, Irish people mostly made their living by raising cattle. This meant that in some areas, particularly Ulster, the people were semi-nomadic. Most warfare consisted of cattle raiding, often over long distances, into another kingdom. Irishmen fought without armour, using short spears, javelins or large axes. The Irish had no towns, apart from the Viking trading ports. Because they did not live in towns or farms, the Irish were often despised by English writers. (Source C)

A reconstruction at the Ulster History Park near Omagh, Co. Tyrone of a Celtic monastery.

People who are **nomadic** travel about and don't live in one place for very long.

2.2 Dermot of the Foreigners

The main Irish kingdoms and Viking settlements in 1166.

B

Dermot was tall and well-built, a brave and warlike man among his people, whose voice was hoarse from constantly having been in the din of battle. He was obnoxious to his own people and hated by others. He preferred to be feared than to be loved.

Gerald of Wales, who was half Welsh and half Norman, describing Dermot.

C

Henry, King of England, Duke of Normandy and Aquitaine and Count of Anjou, to all his liegemen, English, Normans, Welsh and Scots, and to all nations subject to his sway sends greetings. Whensoever these our letters shall come to you, know you that we have taken Dermot, prince of the men of Leinster, into the bosom of our grace and good will. Wherefore, too, whosoever within the bounds of our dominions shall be willing to lend aid to him, as being our vassal and liegeman, in the recover of his own, let him know that he has our favour and permission to that end.

Letter given by Henry II to Dermot MacMurrough in 1167.

Dermot and the Normans

Dermot Mac Murrough was the King of Leinster. He is one of the most controversial people in Irish history, because Irish writers called him 'Diarmait na nGall' - meaning he was the man who brought the foreigners to Ireland. In other words he is regarded as responsible for bringing the English into Ireland.

This is not strictly true. Several Norman influences were to be seen in Ireland before the first knights arrived in 1169. Dermot was only one of a number of Irish rulers who had begun to copy the fashions of the Normans in clothes and behaviour. Irish trade was already in the control of the Vikings. St. Malachy, Archbishop of Armagh had set up Cistercian (French style) abbeys at Mellifont and Jerpoint.

Dermot and the High King

Dermot had been an ally of the King of Tyrone, the previous High King. Dermot had hoped to be High King himself one day, but he had much to fear from Rory O'Connor becoming High King (page 20). Rory encouraged Dermot's sub-kings in Leinster to desert him. When O'Connor invaded Leinster in 1166 Dermot went to his Norman friends in Wales to seek help. Wales had already been occupied by the Normans (see Unit 2.6) and the Welsh archers were much admired. What Dermot wanted was to recruit **mercenaries** to help him recover his Kingdom.

Dermot and Henry II

Dermot's Norman friends were unwilling to offer help unless Dermot first got the approval of their King, Henry II. Henry was fighting a war in France so Dermot travelled there to see him. Dermot knew the way the feudal system worked (see Unit 3.1). He swore loyalty to Henry as his **overlord**, in effect making him High King. In return Henry would have to give him protection as a **vassal**. With letters of support from Henry II, Dermot returned to Wales, and recruited a Norman army. This army began to arrive in Ireland in 1169.

D

Dermot MacMurrough.

E

See how the enemy of his country, that despot over his own people and universal enemy, previously driven from his country, has now returned flanked by the arms of foreigners, to bring about our common ruin.

Part of a speech by Rory O'Connor in 1170, quoted by Gerald of Wales.

A **mercenary** is a soldier who fights for anyone in return for money.

An **overlord** is someone who rules over another.

A **vassal** holds land belonging to a lord and owes the lord loyalty and service.

?

1 Look at Unit 3.1. Why was it so important for Dermot to have Henry II as an overlord?

2 "Dermot brought the foreigners to Ireland". Using the evidence in this Unit explain why you agree or disagree with this statement.

3 Study Source C. What places did Henry II claim to rule over?

2.3 The Coming of Strongbow

The marriage of Strongbow and Aoife, painted in the 19th century.

B

We are restoring the fortunes of this honourable man, our excellent and generous benefactor, who has been cheated by the treachery of his own people.

Fitzstephen speaking of Dermot, 1169, quoted by Gerald of Wales.

C

Perhaps the outcome of this present action will be that the five divisions of the island will be reduced to one, and the sovereignty over the whole kingdom will devolve upon our race in the future.

Fitzstephen, as above.

D

It is not, then, greed for monetary rewards or the 'blind craving for gold' that has brought us to these parts, but a gift of lands and cities in perpetuity to us and to our children.

Fitzstephen, as above.

The First Normans

Dermot had gone to seek help in 1166, but it was to be three years before the first Normans arrived, in 1169. Meanwhile O'Connor, the High King, had allowed Dermot to keep a small bit of land near Wexford. It was here that the first Normans landed in May 1169 with fewer than 400 men. But why did these men come? Did they do it for money or for some other reason? Look at Sources B - D and decide for yourself. Most of the knights who came to Ireland had no land of their own in Wales. In fact Fitzstephen had been held prisoner by the Welsh before coming to Ireland.

This first batch of Normans captured Wexford from the Vikings. O'Connor was so impressed by this success that he made peace with Dermot and restored to him the Kingship of Leinster. Dermot promised to bring no more foreigners to Ireland, but soon broke his word. Maurice Fitzgerald arrived in August 1169 with more Normans, and in May 1170 **Strongbow** himself arrived.

E

In this way the victory was won, and about 200 heads of his enemies were laid at Dermot's feet. When he had turned each one over and recognised it ... he jumped 3 times in the air with arms clasped over his head. He lifted up to his mouth the head of one he particularly loathed, and taking it by the ears and hair, gnawed at the nose and cheeks - a cruel and most inhuman act.

Gerald of Wales, describing Dermot's behaviour after a battle in 1169

The Normans who came to fight for Dermot

Date	Name	Knights	Men at Arms	Archers and Footsoldiers	Totals
May 1169	Fitzstephen	30	60	300	390
Aug 1169	Fitzgerald	10	—	130	140
May 1170	Raymond le Gros	10	—	70	80
Aug 1170	Strongbow	200	—	1000	1200
Totals		250	60	1500	1810

Strongbow captures Dublin

Richard de Clare (Strongbow) was a very important Welsh Norman. He had lost his land, and Henry II half promised that he could make up for this by getting land in Ireland. He landed in 1170 with a considerable force of 1200 men, 200 of them knights. He and Dermot captured Waterford and then marched North and captured Dublin. Strongbow married Dermot's eldest daughter Aoife (pronounced 'Eefa') and Dermot promised that when he died, Strongbow would become King of Leinster. Dermot now had plans to defeat O'Connor and make himself High King, but he died suddenly in 1171 and Strongbow declared himself King of Leinster. O'Connor now realised what a threat Strongbow was so he attempted to recapture Dublin by allying himself with the Vikings from the Isle of Man and the western isles of Scotland, as well as all the other Irish Kings.

This army, estimated at 30 000, surrounded Dublin, which was defended by only about 2000 Normans. They were defeated when the Normans made a surprise attack on the Irish/Viking camp. O'Connor was having a bath in his tent at that moment, and had to make a run for it, presumably still wet! As a result of the battle, Strongbow was King of Leinster, and controlled the trading ports of Dublin, Wexford and Waterford.

F

Dermot MacMurrough, King of Leinster, by whom a trembling sod was made of all Ireland, after bringing over the Saxons, after having done extensive injury to the Gael, after plundering and burning many churches at Kells, Clonard etc., died at Ferns before the end of the year after this plundering, by an insufferable and unknown disease, through the miracles of God, Columba and Finnan, whose churches he had profaned some time before, without will, without penance, without the body of Christ, as his evil deeds deserved.

An account by monks in Donegal of the year 1171 AD

?

1. Would you regard the painting (Source A) as a primary or secondary source? Give reasons for your answer.

2. In your own words list the reasons Fitzstephen gives for coming to Ireland (Sources B - D).

3. How does the monk in Source F explain Dermot's death?

4. How did Rory O'Connor react to the Normans (a) in 1169 and (b) in 1171?

2.4 Henry II comes to Ireland

The purpose of this unit is to study *why* Henry II came to Ireland and to look at the results of his visit. Henry II had several reasons for coming.

1 As early as 1154, when Henry II became king, he had ambitions to add Ireland to his **dominions**.

2 In 1155, the Pope (Adrian IV) had given his blessing to Henry II coming to Ireland. This was because the Irish church was not yet under the control of the Pope, so Henry would 'enlarge the boundaries of his church' (see Source A). Incidentally this Pope was an Englishman. Might this have helped?

3 When Dermot came to Henry in 1167 (Unit 2.2), this gave Henry the opportunity he needed to get a foothold in Ireland.

4 By 1171 Henry II was in bad favour with the new Pope (Alexander III) because Henry's knights in 1170 had murdered Thomas Becket, the Archbishop of Canterbury. Henry hoped to make up for this crime by invading Ireland and, giving the Pope control over the Irish church.

5 Henry was alarmed and angered by Strongbow taking the title **King of Leinster** and decided to come to Ireland to show who was boss, so to speak. (Source B)

A
Adrian, bishop, servant of the servants of God, to our beloved son in Christ the illustrious King of the English, greeting .... as becomes a Catholic prince, your purpose to enlarge the boundaries of the Church, to proclaim the truths of the Christian religion to a rude and ignorant people ..... we therefore do declare our will and pleasure that, with a view to enlarging the boundaries of the Church .... you shall enter that island and execute (carry out) whatsoever may tend to the honour of God and the welfare of that land ..

From the Papal Bull *Laudabiliter*, by which Pope Adrian IV granted Ireland to King Henry II in England in 1155.

B
When these [Strongbow's] successes had become known to the King of England, he was moved to anger against the earl for having attempted so great an enterprise, not only without consulting him but even in defiance of him, and also because the Earl had taken to himself the glory of so noble a conquest, which ought rather to have been given to the king as his superior.

William of Newburgh *The History of England* 1197

The Arrival of Henry II

Strongbow realised that by becoming a king he had gone too far. He met Henry in Wales and made his peace. He renewed his oath of homage, and handed over all the lands he had conquered. In October 1171 Henry II arrived in Ireland with a considerable force of 250 ships, 500 knights, and up to 4000 archers and foot soldiers. Both Irish and Normans had good reason to be scared. All the Norman lords submitted to him in Dublin. Strongbow was granted Leinster, but as a lord, not a king. **Hugh de Lacy** was appointed as the King's representative in Ireland. Henry kept Dublin, Wexford and Waterford for himself.

C

Rock of Cashel, Co. Tipperary, where the Kings of Munster were traditionally crowned. The Irish bishops met here in 1172.

Dominions are lands and countries that a king rules over.

The Irish Kings deserted Rory O'Connor and rushed to Dublin to recognise Henry II as their lord. Early in 1172 the Irish bishops and abbots met at **Cashel**, and promised to bring the Irish church into line with the rest of Europe, and to fully recognise the Pope's authority. Henry then returned to England. This helped Henry to make his peace with the Pope. In 1173 Becket was declared a saint (Saint Thomas) and a year later Henry II did penance by walking barefoot through Canterbury, and being whipped by the bishops at Becket's tomb.

Activities

1 Make a timeline of Henry II's involvement in Ireland. You should have entries for 1155, 1167, 1171, 1172, 1175.

2 Make a time line about Henry II and Becket. You should have entries for 1170, 1171, 1173, 1174.

The Norman Conquest continues

Henry II never returned to Ireland, but his knights continued to take land, at the expense of the Irish Kings. De Lacy conquered Meath in 1173. Rory O'Connor made an agreement with Henry in 1175, called the **Treaty of Windsor.** Rory would remain High King of the non-Norman parts of Ireland, in return for a tribute from the kings under him. Despite this, Norman knights like John de Courcy continued to conquer Irish territory (Unit 2.5) and O'Connor's authority collapsed. He was the last Irish High King.

?

1 What 2 reasons had Henry for being angry with Strongbow? (Source B)

2 What do you think Pope Alexander III would think about the outcome of Henry's invasion of Ireland?

3 Was the promise made to O'Connor in the Treaty of Windsor, kept?

CASE STUDY

2.5 John de Courcy and Ulster

We can learn quite a lot about the Normans in Ireland by studying a particular individual. This case study looks at the fortunes of a young Norman knight called **John de Courcy**.

Many stories were told about John. He became a legend even in his own time, so it is hard to tell fact from fiction. In French, *de* means 'of' or 'from', and the de Courcy family came from Courcy in Normandy. John's ancestors had come to England with William the Conqueror in 1066. They were given land in Somerset in southern England. John was a younger son of the family and had no land of his own. He had served King Henry II in his wars in France, and in 1176 he came to Dublin with William FitzAudelin, the new governor.

War provided many young Norman knights with their only real chance of getting land and becoming rich. If they fought bravely and well, the king or someone else might reward them with land from conquered territory. John had been unlucky so far. Henry II had not rewarded him.

The Attack on Ulaid

The death of the King of Tyrone in 1166 (page 20) had resulted in the smaller Ulster kingdoms fighting each other now that there was no strong king to control them. It would seem that **MacDunlevy**, the **King of Ulaid** (modern Antrim and Down) may have copied Dermot MacMurrough (Unit 2.2) by inviting the Normans to come to Ulster and help him fight the other kings.

An artist's impression of John de Courcy.

?
1 Why did John de Courcy decide to leave his home in Somerset?

2 What reasons are suggested in Source D for FitzAudlin's men being discontented?

3 How might a prophecy like Source E have helped de Courcy take over Ulster?

B
John was fair haired and tall, with bony and sinewy limbs. His frame was lanky and he had a very strong physique, immense bodily strength and an extraordinarily bold temperament. He was a man of courage and a born fighter. In war he was impetuous. Away from the battlefield he was modest and restrained, and he gave the church of Christ that honour which is its due.

Gerald of Wales, about 1189

- 28 -

A life size model, in Carrickfergus Castle, of John de Courcy on horseback, attended by a page boy.

De Courcy planned, not just to help MacDunlevy, but to replace him as ruler. To justify his attack, de Courcy used two reasons:

1 He claimed that Henry II, probably at Windsor in 1175, had promised him Ulster "if he could conquer it by force".

2 De Courcy collected prophetic writings, especially ones that might be fulfilled by him. One of these was Source E. He was also white-haired (Source B), and had a white horse (Source C) and a shield with 3 eagles (Source A). Some writers think that de Courcy might have made up some of the prophecies himself.

In 1177, John de Courcy marched 22 knights and about 300 foot soldiers to Ulaid and arrived at Downpatrick. MacDunlevy retreated in fright, but soon recruited a large army from his allies and returned to Downpatrick to give battle. According to one account, he brought priests and monks who stood on a hill to pray for de Courcy's defeat. De Courcy sent his troops to attack the praying monks, and then went on to win the battle!

D

Now John de Courcy saw that FitzAudlin was acting entirely from motives of greed, cowardice and double dealing, and that he was neither trusted by the Normans, nor feared by the Irish. He therefore won over to his side some of the Dublin garrison. They had not been paid for some time, and were discontented because of FitzAudlin's laziness in not filling the money chests with booty from the Irish. John's followers were few in number, but good, brave men, the pick of the army. So with 22 knights and about 300 others, this brave knight boldly made an assault on Ulaid...

Gerald of Wales (adapted) about 1189.

E

A white knight, astride a white horse, bearing a device of birds on his shield will be the first to enter Ulaid and overrun it with hostile intent.

Prophecy by Merlin of Celidon, quoted by Gerald of Wales.

CASE STUDY

Carrickfergus Castle, built by John de Courcy.

De Courcy as Lord of Ulster

Despite having only about 400 soldiers, John de Courcy was able to defeat the local Irish. Probably some Irish were fighting on his side too, but the superior weapons and armour of the Normans helped them to win victories even when outnumbered. De Courcy took over most of Down and Antrim and built castles on its borders. He made **Carrickfergus** his headquarters, and there he built his strongest castle. Today it is very famous and you can read more about it in Units 3.3 and 3.4.

John de Courcy realised how important it was to be accepted as ruler by the local Irish. He used religion to do this. At Downpatrick, the headquarters of MacDunlevy had been a fortified hill, now called **The Hill of Down**.

G

Only someone who was there, and who saw the blows dealt out by John's sword, how it lopped off now a head from someone's shoulders, or again arms or hands from their body, could adequately praise the powers of this valiant warrior.

Gerald of Wales describing John de Courcy at the Battle of Downpatrick, 1177

De Courcy built a castle there and rebuilt the cathedral on a nearby hill. He named the cathedral after St. Patrick. In 1185 de Courcy claimed that the bodies of St. Patrick, St. Columba (Columbcille) and St. Brigid had been discovered there. This made Downpatrick an important religious site. He had coins struck with the head of St. Patrick on one side and his own head on the other. Since only kings were meant to have their heads on coins, what did this suggest? One of these coins is now in **Down County Museum**.

To strengthen himself further, de Courcy (in 1180) married the daughter of Guthred, King of the Isle of Man — she was called Affreca.

Activities

1 Use all the sources in this four page unit to write a description of the appearance and character of John de Courcy.

2 Construct a timeline of the life of John de Courcy

Down Cathedral painted in 1863 by Thomas Semple. De Courcy named this cathedral after St. Patrick. De Courcy's cathedral was rebuilt as shown, in the 19th century.

The Downfall of de Courcy

John de Courcy ruled Ulster for 27 years and in his day was one of the most powerful Normans in Ireland. But the King's son, **Prince John**, was jealous of de Courcy and feared his power. Prince John had been made 'Lord of Ireland' by his father, but de Courcy's coins did not acknowledge John's lordship.

In 1199 Henry II died and John became the king. In 1204 King John ordered **Hugh de Lacy**, the ruler of Meath, to invade Ulster and drive de Courcy out. After a short war, de Courcy fled abroad and lived the rest of his life in relative poverty. De Lacy became Earl of Ulster.

> I
>
> *John de Courcy soon after proceeded to plunder Dalriada [Co. Antrim] and Hy Tuirtre and Firlee gave battle to him and his foreigners and defeated them with great slaughter ... and John himself escaped with difficulty, being severely wounded, and fled to Dublin.*

Annals of the Four Masters 1178, giving an account of a battle in Co. Antrim.

?

1 What evidence can you find in this four page unit to support the claim that John de Courcy was a very religious man?

2 What were the consequences (results) of John de Courcy's invasion of Ulaid?

3 What were the causes of John de Courcy's downfall?

The story of John de Courcy showed that a Norman knight could win land and power very quickly, but that it was important not to make enemies and, above all, to keep the favour of the King. De Courcy started his life with nothing but a name and ended his life the same way.

2.6 Wales and the Normans

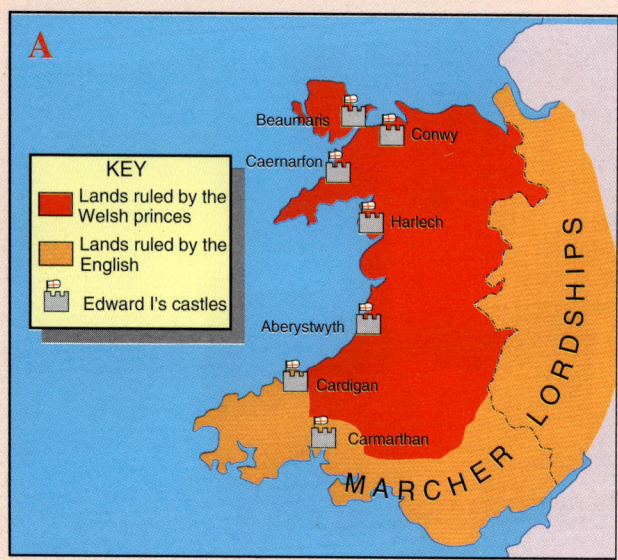

Map of Wales

> **B**
>
> *Their only idea of tactics is either to follow their opponents or else run away from them. They cannot fight violently for very long or try to win a hand-to-hand fight.*
>
> *They may not do well in open fighting but they harass the enemy by ambushes and night attacks, In a single battle, they are easily beaten, but they are difficult to conquer in a long war, for they are not troubled by hunger or cold, fighting does not seem to tire them, they do not lose heart when things go wrong, and after one defeat they are ready to fight again and to face once more the hazards of war.*

Gerald of Wales, *Description of Wales*, 1194.

Wales is a land of mountains and valleys, surrounded on three sides by the sea. The Welsh had their own language and were descended from the Celts who had lived in Britain before the Saxons came. The Welsh had fought the Saxons long before the Normans arrived. The Normans soon invaded Wales and took over land in the south and the east along the English border. These areas were known as the **marches**, and the Normans who lived there as **marcher lords**. The Welsh adapted well to the Norman conquest and Welsh archers served in the Norman armies that came to Ireland in 1170.

The northern Welsh were less easily subdued. They copied the English weapons and castles, but when the English were weakened by civil or foreign war, they rebelled. The most famous Welsh leader was Llywelyn the Great (1173-1240) who dreamed of a united independent Wales. But in 1272 Edward I, a very strong English King came to the throne. He conquered Wales and built 17 new stone castles at Carmarthen, Harlech, Beaumaris and other places. They were the biggest and most impressive castles to be built in Britain. Edward's eldest son was declared **Prince of Wales**.

Harlech Castle, north Wales, built in 1283 - 89. The green area on the left was sea in 1283.

?
1. Study Source B. List (a) the good points and (b) the bad points Gerald makes about the Welsh.

2. Would the other information on this page suggest that the Normans agreed or disagreed with him?

2.7 Scotland and the Normans

Scotland was the last part of the British Isles to be invaded by the Normans and their successors. Scotland had its own kings and the Western Isles were ruled by Vikings from Norway. In the 12th century the Scots had even invaded the north of England. Sometimes the English kings tried to get the king of Scotland to do homage to them for the throne of Scotland.

In the 13th century the Scottish kings became more powerful and took over the Viking areas. They were crowned at **Scone**, near Perth, on a special stone which was supposed to have come from the Holy Land and to have been Jacob's pillow when he had the dream about the ladder reaching up to Heaven. (Genesis 28 verse 11)

In 1286 King Alexander III died with no heir, and the Scots asked King Edward I of England to pick a new king for them. This was a big mistake. It allowed Edward I to meddle in Scotland. He invaded Scotland three times and stole the **Stone of Scone**. It is now in Westminster abbey under the Royal throne. The Scots fought England fiercely, led first by **William Wallace** and then by **Robert the Bruce**.

In 1314 Scottish independence was secured when Robert the Bruce defeated Edward II at the **Battle of Bannockburn**. This victory led the Irish to invite Bruce to come to Ireland and help them fight the Normans. Robert's brother Edward arrived in 1315 and won control of Ulster. He was crowned King of Ireland near Dundalk in 1316, but his success was short lived because he was killed in battle in 1318.

A

For, as long as a hundred of us remain alive, we will never ... be subjected to the lordship of the English.

From the *Declaration of Arbroath*, 1320

B

Scotland in the 13th and 14th centuries

KEY
- Norwegian until 1266
- Scotland before 1266
- X Battle

C

For in this Bruce's time, for three years and a half, falsehood and famine and killing filled the country and undoubtedly men ate each other in Ireland.

Edward Bruce's invasion of Ireland. From *The Irish Annals*

Activity

Write notes on the following:
The Stone of Scone;
Robert the Bruce;
Edward Bruce.

3.1 The Feudal System

Today most farmers own the land they farm or else rent it from someone else for money. In the Middle Ages it didn't work like that. No one *owned* land except the King and the Church. Everyone else *held* their land in exchange for duties and services (not money). If they did not carry out the duties, the land was taken from them. This is called the **Feudal System**.

It worked something like this:

KING

Land granted **BARONS/BISHOPS** about 200 Must provide knights and men for the King

Land granted **KNIGHTS** about 2000 Must fight for the Baron and provide armed men

Farmland granted **PEASANTS** about 1.5 million Must fight for the knight and work on his land, etc.

The King

The King was the top of the Feudal System. It made it easy for him to control his barons. He granted them a lot of land in return for an oath of fealty (Source A). If they rebelled against him the oath was broken and he could take the land back.

Barons

Barons had to appear at court, pay taxes to the King, and supply 20-30 fully armed knights and about 400 foot soldiers in time of war. Feudalism was how the King got an army. Each baron had land equal to about 500 square kilometres, usually scattered in several places. They in turn gave land to about 20-30 knights in return for an oath of fealty from them.

Knights

A knight had to fight for his lord and supply about 20 foot soldiers as well. He also had to supply food and money to the baron. The knight in his turn usually controlled a town or village and got these things from his peasants, who had to be loyal to him. Some knights had no land but hoped to be rewarded with land if they fought well.

Peasants

Peasants (or **villeins**) depended on the knight for their land. They had to be loyal to him, fight for him in time of war, and carry out lots of duties (see Source B). These didn't leave a lot of time for working on their own land. The big advantage was that your knight had to protect you if you were threatened by another baron or knight. You might have to pay taxes to the King. By the late Middle Ages, many peasants were being paid to work on the lord's land. (Unit 3.11)

The Church

The King directly owned about a quarter of England (mostly the forests), and the barons about half. The remaining quarter was owned by the Church, mostly by abbeys (see Unit 3.9), and so many villeins worked for an abbot instead of a knight or baron. In return the Church helped the King to run the country, and taught everyone to obey the King and barons.

A

I become your man from this day forward, for life and limb and loyalty. I shall be true and faithful to you for the lands I hold from you.

Oath taken in Norman times by anyone who received land from someone.

B

Adam Underwood holds 30 acres of his lord, the Earl of Warwick, and in return he has to give the following dues and services:

1 Work every Monday, Wednesday and Friday from October to August. Work 2 days a week from August to October. This can be ploughing, haymaking, harvesting, carting stones and gathering nuts.

2 Leave his own land at haymaking and harvest time and work for his lord.

3 Make gifts of oats, a hen and food for 3 horses, 12 pence at Christmas, 1 penny for every pig a year old and a half a penny for younger ones.

Domesday Book 1086; entry for Brailes, Warwickshire

Dues are money or other gifts you had to give your lord.

Fealty means faithfulness or loyalty.

A **villein** was a peasant who was not a slave.

To do **homage** means to show humility to the person over you.

3.2 Castles 1: Motte and Bailey

An artist's reconstruction of the motte and bailey castle at Clough, Co. Down, around 1200

If the Normans depended on their mounted knights and their armour to *win* control of England, Ireland and Wales, they depended on their castles to *keep* control of them.

The earliest castles had to be built quickly. It could take 10 years to build a stone castle, so the earliest castles were wooden. These wooden castles are called **motte and bailey castles**. The people the Normans had just conquered were usually forced to build the castles.

B

He [William I] *caused castles to be built which were a sore burden to the poor.*

Anglo-Saxon Chronicle 1087

Activity

Divide the class into attackers and defenders of Clough Castle. One group plans the defence of the Castle and the other the attack.

Clough Castle, near Downpatrick, as it is today. The bailey is the earthwork on the right.

- 36 -

D

When the King was informed that the people of the north had gathered together and would oppose him if he came, he marched to Nottingham and built a castle there, and so on to York, and there built two castles, and also in Lincoln, and in many other places in that part of the country.

Anglo-Saxon Chronicle 1068

A Norman knight has just ridden into the castle. (From an original painting at the Ulster History Park, Omagh.)

The main parts of a motte and bailey castle were:

- **1 The Motte.** This was a small hill or earthwork made by digging a large circular ditch and throwing the soil up in the centre.
- **2 The Keep.** This was a tower built on the top of the motte as a lookout. Sometimes, as at Clough, the wooden keep might be replaced by a stone keep.
- **3 The Bailey.** This was an enclosed area, usually on a smaller earthwork than the motte. Here the soldiers lived and slept.
- **4 The Moat.** This is the name given to the deep ditch surrounding the whole castle. *Sometimes*, but not often, it was filled with water.
- **5 Wooden Bridge.** This connected the keep to the bailey. Defenders smashed it if they had to retreat to the keep.

The Ulster History park near Omagh, Co. Tyrone, contains a full size replica of a motte and bailey castle.

?

1 Identify the parts of the castle marked A - E in Source A.

2 What do Sources B and D suggest about the effects of castle building?

3 Source C is an actual motte at Clough, Co. Down. Source A is an artist's reconstruction of the same motte as it would have looked in 1200. Explain the advantages each would have in helping you to understand this type of castle.

4 What parts of a motte and bailey castle are shown in (a) Source E and (b) Source F?

3.3   Castles 2:   Monuments in Stone

As soon as they could, the Normans began to replace their motte and bailey castles with stone castles. Early castles were still built on mottes, and square cornered towers were common. Later the Crusaders went to the Holy Land and copied new castle building techniques. Round towers and concentric castles with machicolations became more common. The commonest type of castle was the **keep in bailey castle**. This had a stone keep surrounded by a curtain wall. Sometimes the keep formed part of the outer wall. Keep in bailey castles were built mostly in the 12th and 13th centuries. Carrickfergus Castle is an example.

Embrasure (space)   **Merlon** (wall between spaces)   **Wall walk**

The roof of the keep at Castle Rushen, Castletown, Isle of Man. This shows the wall walk very clearly.

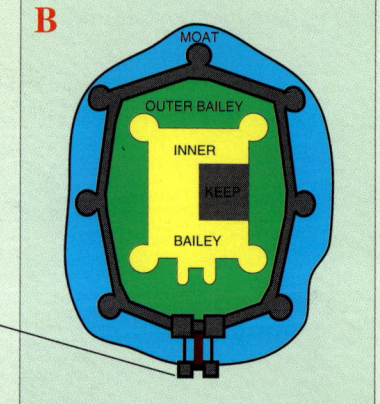

Barbican (outer defensive entrance, outside the moat)

Diagram of a **concentric castle**. This was a castle with two curtain walls and an inner and outer bailey. The inner curtain wall is higher than the outer. An example is Beaumaris Castle in Wales. These were usually built in the 14th century. They are almost unknown in Ireland, but there are many examples in England and Wales.

Curtain Wall   **Gatehouse** (both towers and central arch)   **Portcullis** (this could be lowered to close the entrance)   **Drawbridge**

A castle entrance. This commercially produced cardboard model is available from Usborne Publishing.

Crenellations (embrasures + merlons)   **Battlements** (wall used for fighting on)   **Arrow loops** (slit window from which an arrow could be fired)

The keep at Carrickfergus Castle viewed from the wallwalk on the curtain wall. Note the man-at-arms and the archer.

E

Machicolations
(holes in a battlement or wall walk from which missiles or liquids could be dropped)

Third floor — sleeping area

Second floor — eating and entertainment

First floor — kitchen area

Dungeon — for storage

Spiral staircase

?

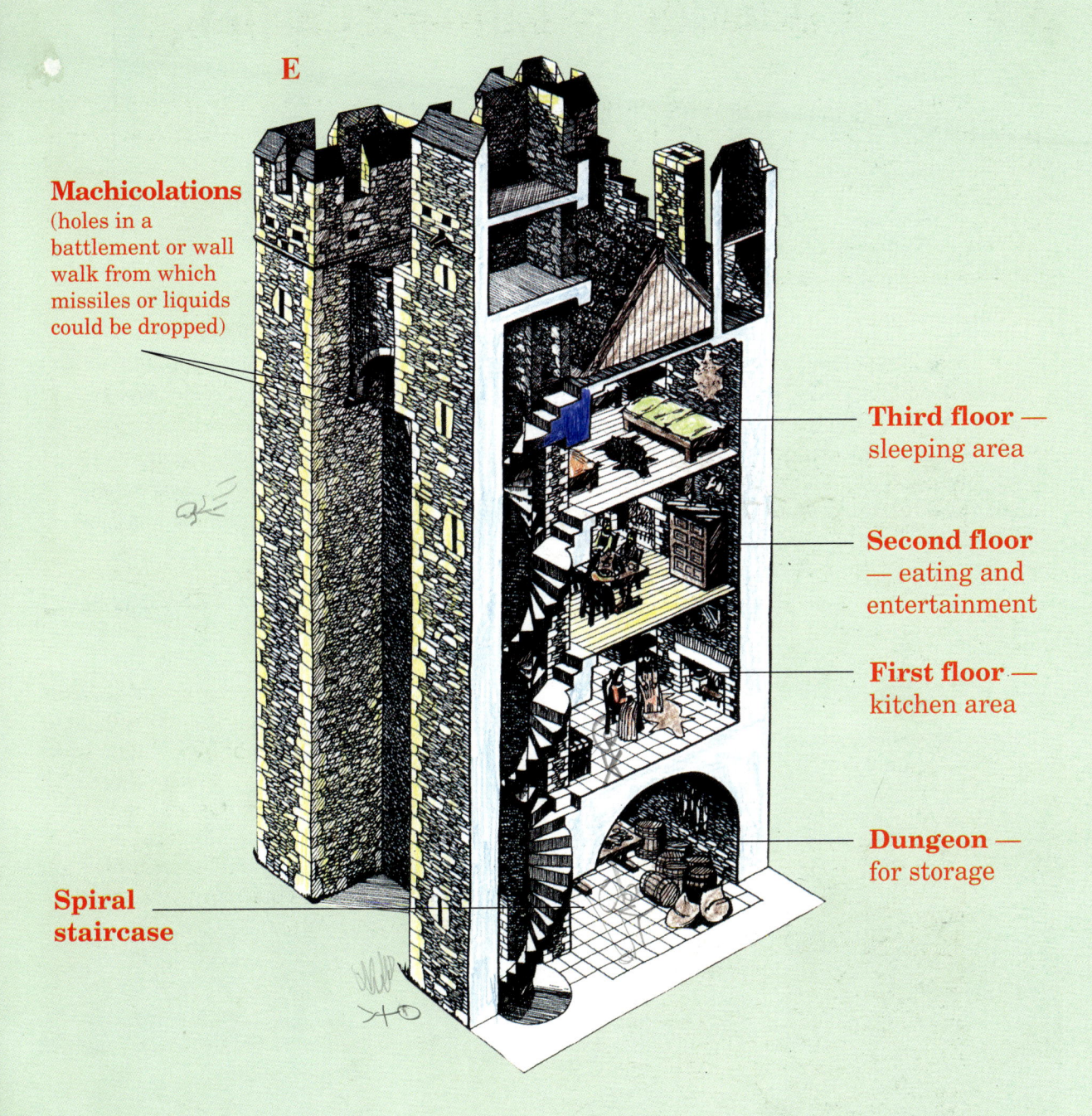

1. Look closely at Source E. What does this tell us about life in a tower house? What features could be used to defend this castle, and how?

2. Why were gateways well defended? What are the defensive features of the gateway in Source C?

The drawing above is of Jordan's Castle in Ardglass, Co. Down. This is a **tower house** and is a good example of the 'gatehouse' type of keep. This is the commonest type of castle in Ireland. A tower house has no curtain wall at all and consists only of a keep. Most have four floors. They were built mostly in the 15th century.

3.4 Castles 3: Life in a Castle

What was it like to live in a castle? Today it is possible to visit many real castles and get some idea of what they were like. Three castles which have furniture and are well worth visiting are:

Carrickfergus Castle, Co. Antrim

Jordan's Castle, Ardglass, Co. Down

Bunratty Castle, Co. Clare

All of the pictures in this unit are from **Carrickfergus Castle**. Since castles were really defensive buildings, they were not very comfortable to live in. They were cold, damp, and draughty. Today the windows usually have glass in them, but in the Middle Ages castle windows had only shutters. The keep of a castle usually contained the living quarters, and Jordan's Castle in Unit 3.3 is fairly typical.

A

We give [to Canterbury Cathedral]... *our chamber hangings of black tapestry with a red border and swans with the heads of ladies ... The blue clothing with golden roses and ostrich feathers we give to our son Richard, together with the bed that we have of the same suite and all the apparel* [bedclothes] *of the said bed which our father the King gave us ...*

From the will of Edward the Black Prince, 1376.

Right: The great hall set for a banquet. The lord sat on the raised platform at the end of the room. Walls were decorated with tapestries. Long trestle tables were set up specially for the occasion.

B

King John in the 'john!' Toilets in medieval castles were usually in the corners of towers. A hole ran through the stonework to the outer wall. Sometimes clothes were hung over toilets in the belief that the smell kept away moths. The toilet was thus called the 'garderobe'.

C

D

Left: The fireplace in the great hall. Note the brackets for torches. The great hall was the most important room in a castle. It had a tall ceiling and was used for banquets and entertainment like dances. The lord held court here too. Sometimes there was a small gallery for musicians. During the day everyone ate in the great hall, and at night most of the soldiers and servants slept here on straw.

Food

Breakfast: bread soaked in ale or watered wine.

Main meal (11.00 a.m.): Mostly meat — usually beef and mutton, sometimes venison and poultry.

Common vegetables: dried peas and beans, onions, garlic, herbs.

Banquets: Meat was often served from the table, and eaten with the hands. Forks were almost unknown. Manners were terrible. You could throw used bones on the floor and it was O.K. to burp!

Ladies

The lord's wife and his daughters and relatives were very important in a castle. They usually had their own private rooms. Since most entrances had curtains and no doors, beds were fitted with curtains. You undressed by kneeling on the bed with the curtains drawn round you. Most women in a castle had to spin and weave cloth. If the lord was away, his lady was responsible for running the castle. High ranking women had their own ladies in waiting.

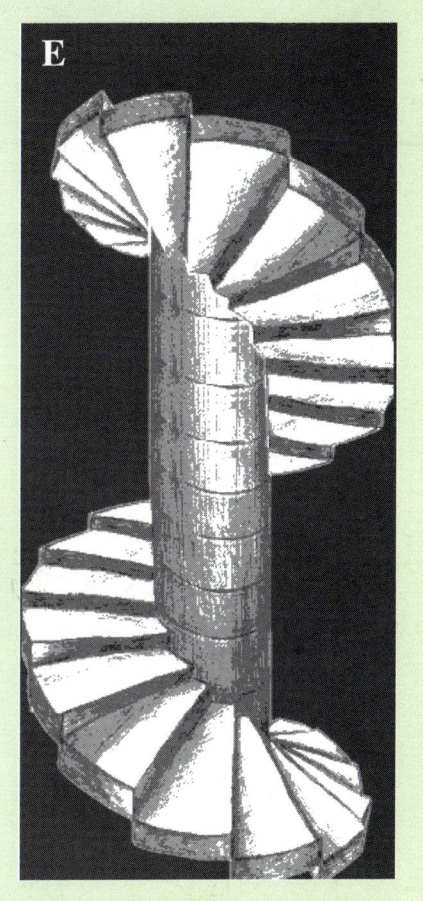

E

To save space, staircases were spiral and built into a corner. Going up, they went clockwise. How did this help a defender? (Clue: swords were usually carried in the right hand.)

F

Castles usually needed a steward to look after the day to day running. Here the steward of Carrickfergus Castle is seen doing his accounts with a quill pen.

Activity

Use the sources in this unit and unit 3.3 to describe a typical day in a medieval castle. (Attacks on castles were *very rare*!)

?

1 What can we learn from Source A about the possessions of a lord?

2 What was the ground floor of a keep used for? (See page 39)

3 How did a spiral staircase help the defender of a castle?

4 Think of as many reasons as you can for castles being uncomfortable to live in.

3.5 Medieval Warfare

A

Medieval jousting being staged at Littlecote Manor, Berkshire, in 1988. The knights carry a traditional lance, used to transfix opponents, but blunted for jousting. (Source B)

B

The two knights spurred forward and met this time with straight lances, hitting each other clean and hard on their shields. Both were nearly knocked to the ground, but they gripped their horses with their legs and stayed on ... This joust was very highly applauded and both French and English said (they) had jousted admirably, without either sparing themselves or causing each other an injury.

Froissart *Chronicles* about 1370.

Knights

In the Middle Ages, knights had to be available for 40 days of military service a year. A fully armed knight needed a lance, shield, sword, horse and full armour. In Norman times the basic armour was a **hauberk** (long coat) of chain mail, and a metal **helmet**. As time went on, armour became more complex. Plate armour replaced mail, and every part of the body was covered. A full suit could weigh 27 kilogrammes. If a knight in full armour fell over, often he could not get up again! Some knights fought with a **mace** which was a hand held weapon about 50 cms long, with a heavy metal ball at one end, often with spikes. It was used to smash an opponents skull or his arm. Odo is using one on page 19.

Knights had a special code of conduct. They had to fight fairly and be polite and protective to ladies. These rules did not apply to ordinary soldiers.

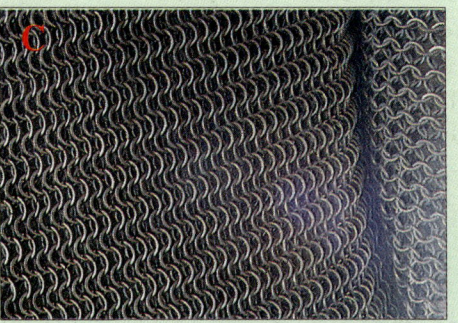

C

Chain mail — there could be as many as 200,000 links in a hauberk.

D

Again in this year it was advised and decreed that throughout the realms of England, no man should use any play or pastime save only the longbow and arrows, on pain of death, and that every bow-maker and arrow-maker should have his debts cancelled.

Froissart *Chronicles* about 1370.

?

1. What weapons were carried by (a) a knight (b) a man at arms (c) an archer?
2. What were the advantages of using the crossbow instead of the longbow?
3. Longbow men were the most valued soldiers in the 14th century. How does this knowledge help us understand Source D?
4. If you were making models like those in Sources E, F and H, how would you get the information needed to be accurate?

SIEGE WARFARE

A **trebuchet** was a large siege 'engine' used to fling heavy stones against castle walls. It worked like a large see-saw. Weights, or people pulling on ropes, brought one side down suddenly and the other side had a sling which flung the stone.

A **catapult** was like the trebuchet. It fired a heavy stone, but was worked by tensioned ropes, instead of counterweights.

A **siege tower** was used to reach the top of a castle or a town wall. Soldiers crossed from the top of the tower to the wall, on a ramp. It was used in Europe and on the Crusades but not in the British Isles.

Guns were not used in the Middle Ages until about 1326. The earliest **cannon** fired *stone* balls, not iron.

BOWS

The **short bow** was used by the Normans in 1066 and on into the 12th century. The bow was about 1.2 metres long and had a range of 250 metres.

The commonest bow in the later Middle Ages was the **long bow**. It was about 2 metres long and had a range of 300 metres. You had to be very strong to use it, so early training was necessary. (Source D)

The **crossbow** was held horizontally and shot bolts (heavy short arrows). The string had to be wound back with a windlass and could fire with a high velocity. It took 12 times as long to reload as a long bow. Useful for defending a castle as it was very accurate.

A 14th century man at arms, guarding the entrance to Carrickfergus castle.

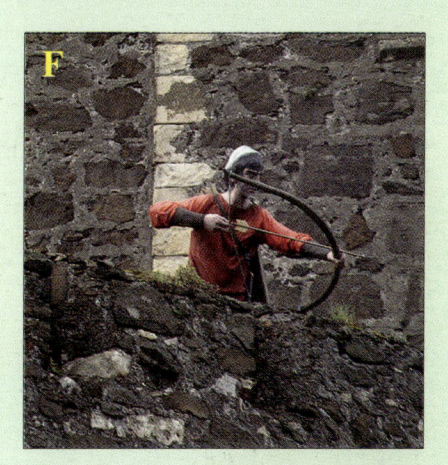

Full size model of an archer on the battlements of Carrickfergus Castle.

A Trebuchet

A crossbow man, Carrickfergus Castle.

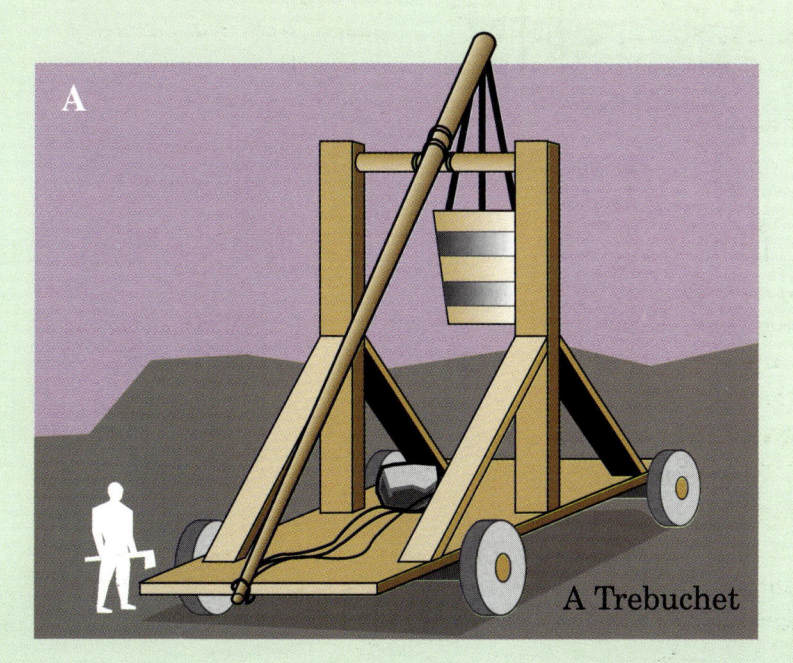

3.6 The Medieval Village

A

(The Bayeux Tapestry - 11th century. By special permission of the City of Bayeux.)

Bayeux Tapestry: Ploughing

In the Middle ages most people lived in a village. There might be 20 or 30 families living in a village, as well as a knight or lord. The most important buildings in a village were the church, the manor house and the mill. The lord of the manor controlled everything that happened in the village, and the villagers had to do what he said. For example they had to ...

- ... work several days a week on his land;
- ... marry the person he told them to;
- ... use only fallen wood for their fires.

Farming

The land belonging to a village was strictly controlled. The land used for growing crops was usually divided into 2 or 3 huge fields (often up to 200 acres, or 1 square kilometre). These fields were called **open fields** as no fences or hedges ran across them. Other land was used to grow hay for the winter, and there was uncultivated **common land** where everyone had the right to graze animals.

On the edges of the village was the forest. Here pigs could be grazed and firewood could be collected — but *not* cut from trees. Peasants could also gather nuts, berries, herbs and wild honey.

The large open fields were divided into long narrow **strips** and each peasant could have 2 - 4 strips in each field. The strips were not always side by side and a lot of time was wasted going from one strip to another. Between each strip was a ditch and this wasted valuable land. Everyone had to grow the same crop in each field, so the system discouraged peasants from trying something different.

B

His coat was of coarse material; his hood was full of holes and his hair stuck out of it. As he trod the soil his toes stuck out of his worn shoes with their thick soles; his stockings hung about his shins on all sides and he was covered with mud as he followed the plough. He had two mittens, scantily made of rough stuff, with worn out fingers and thick with muck.

Description of a ploughman, from *Piers Ploughman* by William Langland, about 1390 (adapted).

C

Let her go often into the fields to see how they are working ... and let her make them get up in the morning. If she be a good housewife, let her rise herself ... go to the window and shout until she sees them come running out, for they are given to laziness.

Duties of a good wife, from *The Goodman of Paris*, 1393

D

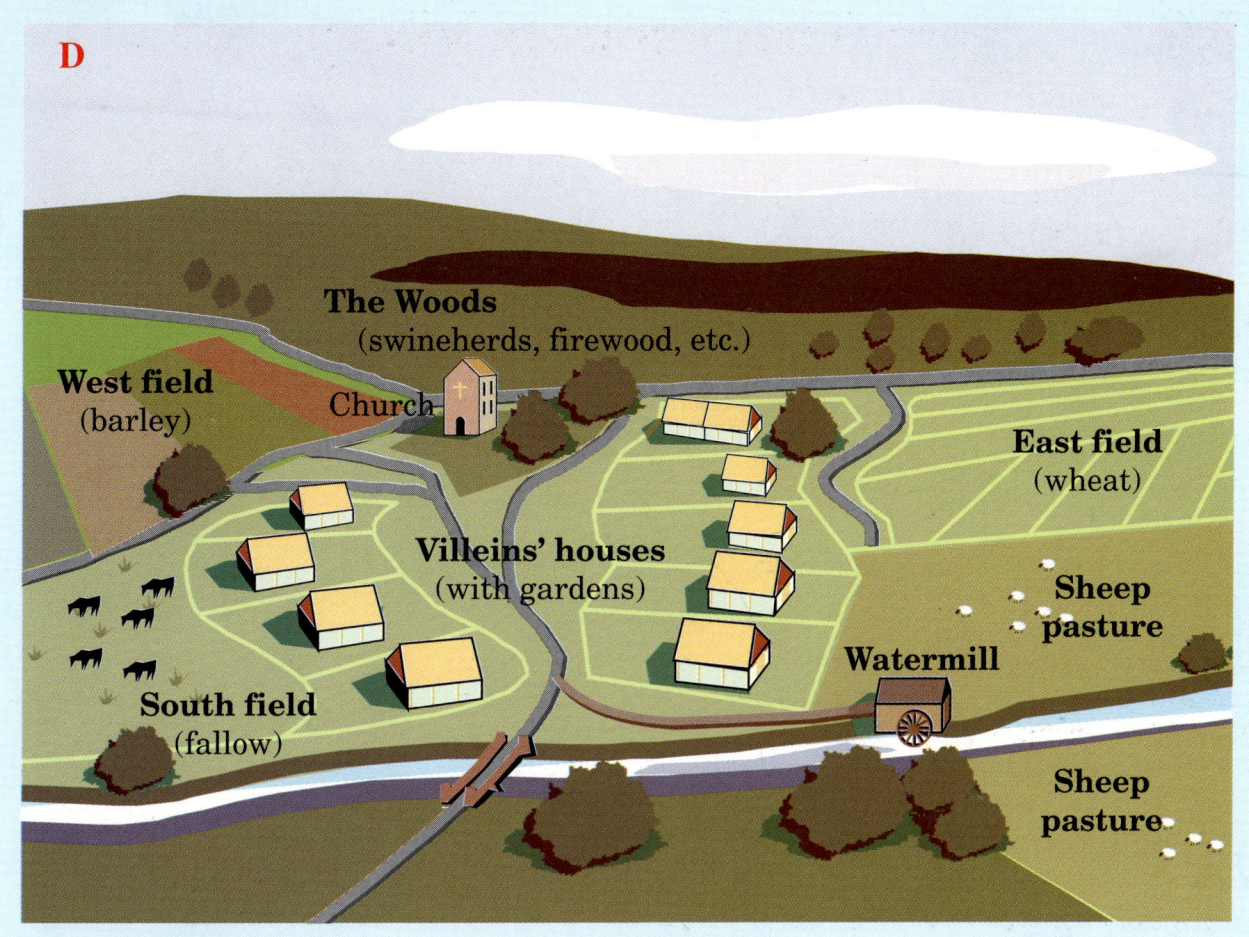

Plan of a Medieval Village

E

	West Field	South Field	East Field
1251	Wheat	Barley or Oats	Fallow
1252	Barley or Oats	Fallow	Wheat
1253	Fallow	Wheat	Barley or Oats
1254	Wheat	Barley or Oats	Fallow
1255	Barley or Oats	Fallow	Wheat

Medieval 3 field crop rotation.

A **hide** was the amount of land needed to support one family.

Fallow land was land left ploughed over with weeds allowed to grow.

A **wattle** wall or fence was made of wood or branches woven together. It could then be plastered over with a mud mixture called **daub**.

Using all the information in this unit, reconstruct a day in the life of either (a) a ploughman or (b) a peasant woman. Think of what they would wear, what they would eat and how they would spend the day.

F

Bayeux Tapestry: Sowing and harrowing. (The Bayeux Tapestry - 11th century. By special permission of the City of Bayeux.)

G

The King holds Great Faringdon. Harold held it. Then it was assessed at 30 hides. Now it does not pay tax. There is land for 15 ploughs. The King has land for 3 ploughs. 27 villeins have 10 ploughs. There are 10 slaves. A mill with a fishery is worth 35 shillings. 130 acres of meadow; woodland for fencing. In this manor Alfsi has 4 hides and land for 2 ploughs.

From *The Domesday Book*, 1086

H

Reconstruction of a timber framed house in the Ulster History Park near Omagh, Co. Tyrone. Medieval house construction was similar to this.

I

1 No one shall enter the fields with a cart to carry grain after sunset.

2 No one shall enter the fields except at the village entrances.

3 All grain collected in the fields shall be taken out openly through the middle of the town and not secretly by back ways.

Village bye-laws of 1293.

?

1 What were (a) the advantages and (b) the disadvantages of having your land in long strips?

2 What does Source C tell us about the life of women in the Middle Ages?

3 What can we learn from Sources A and F about farming methods in Norman times?

4 Can you explain the reasons for the rules in Source I? (Clue: all grain was harvested together and divided up according to the number of strips each peasant had.)

J

Hole in roof for smoke

Wooden frame

Wattle and daub wall

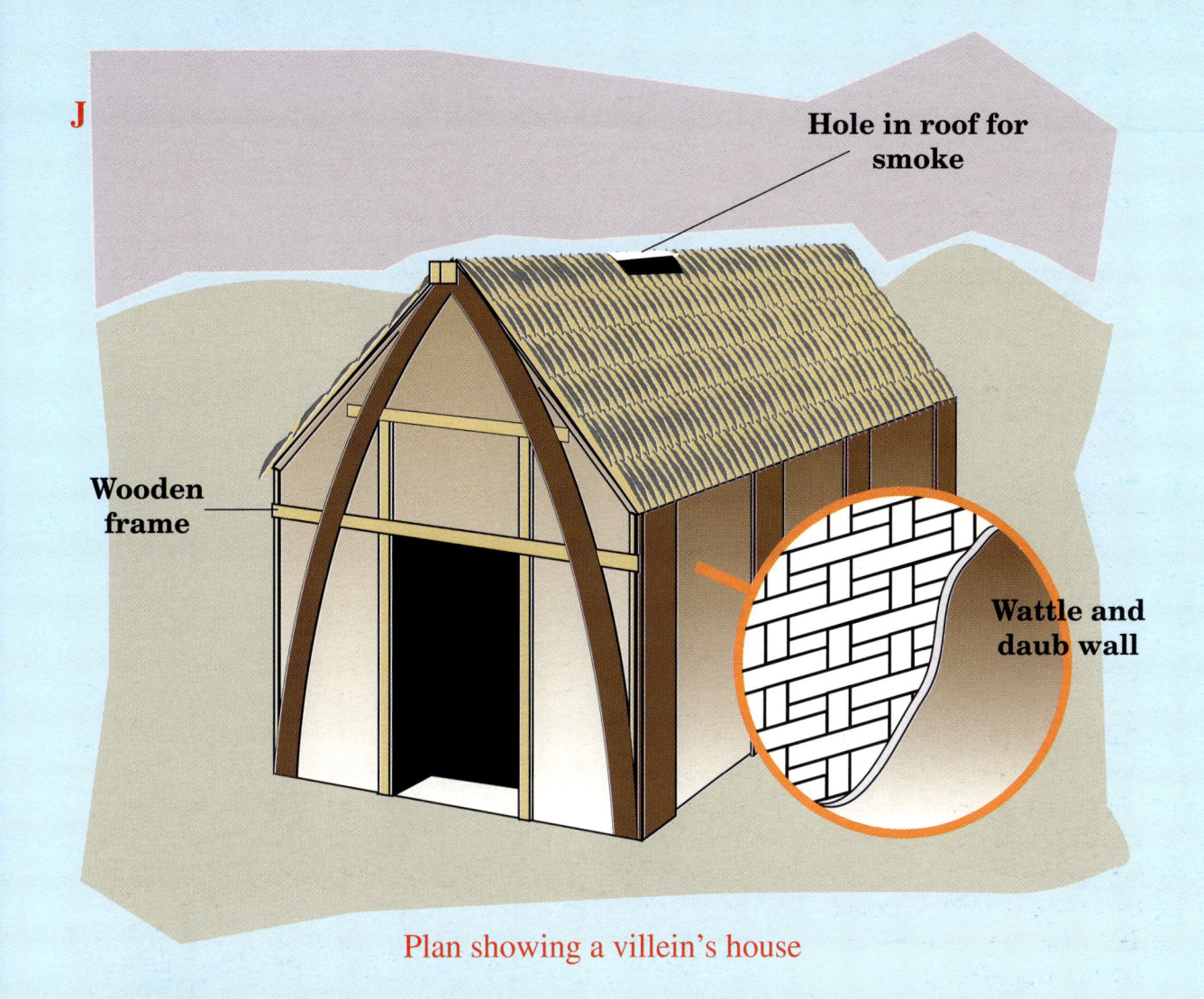

Plan showing a villein's house

Houses

Most ordinary peasants lived in small one-roomed houses. The frame of the house was wooden and the walls were made of **wattle and daub**. Usually there were no windows, only a door. Cooking was done in a pot over an open fire in the middle of the room, and smoke escaped through a hole in the thatched roof. In areas where there was no timber, houses were made of stone.

People lived in one half of the house, and at night animals such as pigs and oxen slept in the other end. There was little furniture — a few three-legged stools, a bench table, and maybe a chest for clothes. The bed was little more than a mattress stuffed with straw.

K

A poor man's income will not stretch to rich food. And though he longs for good ale, he must go to his chill [cold] bedding and lie huddled with his bare head askew [to one side]; and when he tries to stretch his legs, he finds only straw for sheets.

William Langland *Piers Ploughman* about 1390

3.7 The Medieval Town

Towns became very important in the Middle Ages. Most towns were small by modern standards. Only 10 000 people lived in London in Norman times and York had about 5 000. In Ireland the earliest towns were the Viking trading ports of Dublin, Waterford, Cork, etc., or ecclesiastical centres like Armagh. Our study of the medieval town will focus on Irish examples — Carlingford in Co. Louth and Tralee in Co. Kerry. In Tralee the atmosphere of a medieval town has been recreated by a special exhibition called *Geraldine Tralee*, in the Ashe Memorial Hall. Here you can travel back in time and experience, not only the sights, but also the sounds and smells of a medieval town.

A The Leatherworker from Geraldine Tralee. Notice how poor medieval people did not wear very colourful clothing.

B *If any married woman follow a craft within the city, which her husband has nothing to do with, she shall be counted as an unmarried woman in connection with anything to do with her craft. And if a complaint is made against her, she shall answer it as if she were an unmarried woman.*

From the town laws of Lincoln (adapted).

C A street in Carlingford, Co. Louth. This was a Norman settlement. Carlingford still has many features of medieval towns, such as narrow streets, and this tower house, believed to have been a mint.

D *Love and protect your husband and make sure he has clean clothes. His shoes should be taken off in front of a good fire. His feet should be washed and he should have clean shoes and stockings. He should be given good food and drink, and go to bed with white sheets and night caps.*

An old man gives advice to his young wife.

> **E**   *A Charter*
>
> By the grace of God, Henry, King of England, greets you the people of Normanton.
>
> Know ye that I have granted to the people of Normanton all those customs that they enjoyed in the time of my grandfather.
>
> 1. The right of toll. [This allowed the people to charge traders entering the town.]
> 2. The right to hold a market on Tuesdays.
> 3. The right of theam. [This allowed the town to control the courts and keep any fines paid.]
> 4. Freedom for any man who lives in the town for a year and a day without being claimed by his overlord.
>
> Signed this 3rd of October, 1161
>
> Henry II

(Normanton is not a real town)

The Town Walls

Most medieval towns were walled, and there were good reasons for this. Towns were rich and were a temptation to thieves. A wall made the town secure at night, and could keep out other undesirables like diseased people. Town walls were not really designed for defence although a large city might run the risk of attack. A wall was often added when the town was well established and was a status symbol. The townspeople were really saying 'We are important, *we* have a wall round *our* town.'

The walls were usually plain curtain walls with modest gateways like that at Carlingford (Source F). Entry to the town was strictly controlled and tolls were charged to traders. At night the gates were closed and no one was allowed in or out. The town was patrolled by the night watch who kept a lookout for thieves and outbreaks of fire.

The Beginning of Towns

Towns started for many different reasons. In Ireland the earliest towns were ports. Some, like Downpatrick and Armagh, grew up around religious centres. Others, like Carrickfergus and Trim, grew around an important castle. Often a lord of the manor encouraged the development of a town. Tralee was founded by John FitzThomas FitzGerald in 1216, who also established a Dominican Friary.

Lords liked towns because there were more people to pay taxes and if the town had a market, everyone selling merchandise had to pay a tax to the lord. However, as towns developed the townspeople began to resent paying taxes to the lord and often bought their freedom. When a lord gave up control of a town the citizens were granted a **charter** (see Source E). Often these were bought from the king. When a town got its charter it became a **borough** and each citizen who owned a house or business was called a **burgess**. Burgesses could elect a mayor and town council to run the town. They paved the streets, organised a night watch and made regulations about the town.

F

Medieval towns were usually walled. This is a gate tower on the walls around Carlingford. Traders entering through gates to sell in the town had to pay a toll. The building above the gate was the gaol.

G

The Butcher's Stall from Geraldine Tralee. Can you identify the different things the butcher is selling? The woman is wearing a wimple.

H

The Shambles, York — a street of butchers. This is one of the best preserved medieval streets in England. Notice how each floor juts out over the floor below.

Life in the Town

What were medieval towns really like? Firstly they were very small by our standards. Tralee was granted a charter in 1286 and a document dating from 1298 records that the burgesses were paying 100 shillings in annual rent to the Fitzgeralds (Geraldines) who owned the town. This rent suggests that Tralee had a population of 500-600 people. The streets were very narrow. Many of the buildings were timber framed with each floor wider than the one below. If you leaned out far enough through a window you could shake hands with your neighbour across the street! Once a wall was built the town could not get any bigger. Sometimes only the English were allowed to live in the town, and the Irish built houses outside the walls. These settlements were sometimes called **Irishtown**.

Towns were noisy and smelly. Most people threw their rubbish out into the street and emptied their chamber pots straight out of the bedroom window. A narrow drain along the edge of the street carried this away, but only when it rained. Butchers were particularly bad because they threw out offal and rotten meat. The town council often made all the butchers live in one street to keep the problem under control.

Craftsmen and traders usually made the things they sold in small workshops in their own houses. Living above your shop made it easy to keep an eye on things and women often played an active part in the family business or as Source B indicates, might even run their own. Most people just made or sold one thing like shoes, hats, bread, or pies.

I

... covers, blankets, linens, mattresses, painted cloths, rugs, napkins, towels, washbasins, candelabra of bronze, marble and silver gilt, bronze pots and pans, 12 silver spoons, spits, poles, iron pots, vessels of silver-gilt and lead for beer, silver-gilt salt cellars, three iron braziers, and boards for tables, and trestles.

List of contents in a house in Salisbury, from a will of 1410.

Activities

1 Use Sources A, G and J to write a description of how medieval townspeople dressed. Deal separately with women, men and boys.

2 List all the trades mentioned on page 51. Find out what they all did. Find the names of any other trades you know. Which of these names have become surnames?

Law and Order

Dishonesty among traders was a big problem. Some people kept two sets of scales—one for buying and the other for selling! Guess which one over weighed? Others used dangerous ingredients like arsenic or added chalk dust instead of flour to bread. Anyone caught cheating was put in the stocks or the pillory for a day. people then could pelt them with mud, or eggs or empty the chamber pot over them!

Blacksmith's Forge, Geraldine Tralee. What might the blacksmith have bought from the leatherworker? (page 48) What is the man in the background doing?

Craftsmen and Apprentices

Many different trades could be found in a town. These included carpenters, coopers, drapers, embroiderers, glovers, hosiers, furriers, potters, shoemakers, smiths, tailors, and weavers. Different kinds of food were sold by bakers, grocers, vintners, butchers, fishmongers, poulterers, etc.. There were also general merchants who imported unusual goods from England, Europe and even further afield. Merchants often became very rich but the risks were high because of piracy at sea and robbers on land.

In many towns **guilds** controlled all trades. You could only practise a trade if the guild allowed you. The guilds controlled prices charged and the quality of the goods. To enter a trade you had to become an **apprentice**, often at as young as 7, to a master and serve your time for seven years. Once qualified you became a **journeyman**, and now got a wage of several pence a day (The French word for a working day is *journée*). If a journeyman wanted to become independent he had to become a **master craftsman**, but only if the guild allowed. To qualify he had to do a test piece of work, called a **masterpiece**. If he was good enough and if there were not enough in that particular trade, he then became a master.

?

1. Name three places where a town might grow up.

2. Why did townspeople want to buy a charter?

3. List the things that town walls were useful for.

4. Would the evidence in Sources B and D suggest that the social position of women was good or bad?

5. Was the person who wrote the will in Source I rich or poor? Say why.

3.8 The Church

The magnificent west front of the Early English style cathedral at Salisbury in England. Note the tall narrow windows, the lead roof, and the flying buttresses to support the walls.

In the Middle Ages everyone in western and central Europe was Roman Catholic, unless they were Jews. Everyone had to attend church and the church was very powerful. The head of the whole church in Europe was the **Pope** in Rome. He was more powerful than any king and even emperors were supposed to obey him.

The church was very important for ordinary people. There was a church in every village, and it was the centre of their lives. Although the services were in Latin, tapestries, wall hangings and stained glass windows showed vivid images of Heaven, Hell and the demons. Hell was as real to them as their own houses and no one wanted to go there. (Source B)

The church was very wealthy because it owned a quarter of all the land in England. Wealthy nobles and kings often left land to the church so that their souls would be prayed for. The bishops and archbishops were chosen by the Pope and were usually from noble families. Because churchmen understood Latin and were educated, they usually helped the king to rule the country.

The Church and the People

Most people loved the church. Life was full of hardships like famine, disease and poverty. The church brought comfort by offering hope for the future. If you obeyed the priests and did not annoy God, you went to Heaven to be with Christ and his angels. If you were sick, God might heal you.

B

There were trees on fire, and sinners being tortured on those trees. Some were hung by their feet, some by their hair, and some by the arm. There was a furnace of fire burning with seven flames, and many sinners were punished in it. It had a fiery wheel which was turned a thousand times every day by an evil angel. At each turn a thousand sinners were burnt on it.

Description of Hell, by a medieval monk.

C

A boy tried to steal some young pigeons from a nest in Saint David's church. His hand stuck to the stone on which he was leaning. No doubt this was a punishment from the Saint, who was protecting the birds in his own church. For three days and nights the boy, with his parents and friends, prayed at the church altar. On the third day, by God's action, the power which held his hand loosened. He was freed from the force which bound him to the stone. The stone is preserved to this day. The marks of the boy's fingers where he pressed on the stone can be clearly seen, as if it were wax.

Gerald of Wales, describing a 12th century miracle.

The church offered practical help too. Monasteries had to look after the poor by giving out **alms**. They ran the only hospitals and because priests and monks were educated, they ran the only schools.

The church regulated holidays (Holy days) and put on special events like processions and mystery plays. They taught people to obey the king and to respect their lords. Most people believed in real miracles (Source C) and thought that holy relics could heal them.

Church Architecture

The Normans introduced bigger and better churches than had ever been seen before. Until about 1180 churches had windows and doors with rounded arches (See Source B, page 18). Then the **Gothic** style appeared from France, with much thinner walls and pointed arches.

Interior of the restored church at Holy Cross, Co. Tipperary. The window is in the Decorated style, but the walls are thick and typically Norman.

Gothic architecture came in three main phases:

1 **Early English**, about 1180 - 1300. Tall narrow windows were typical.

2 **Decorated**, about 1300 - 1400. Spires were added and large wide windows with geometric patterns were typical.

3 **Perpendicular**, about 1400 - 1550. Very tall buildings. The wide windows had long vertical divisions running from top to bottom.

Churches were often built with the ground plan in the shape of a cross, and with the front of the church facing east. Why do you think builders liked churches to face this way?

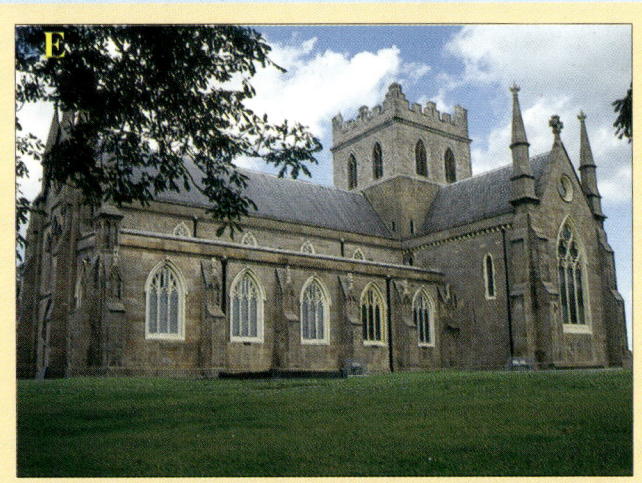

St. Patrick's Church of Ireland Cathedral, Armagh. This is an 18th century restoration of a medieval building. It has a variety of styles. The large south window is Decorated but the five windows in the nave are Perpendicular.

1 What would you like about the church in the Middle Ages if you were (a) an ordinary peasant (b) the king?

2 Study Source B. If you read this in the Middle ages how would you feel about the church?

3 Study Source C. Do you believe this story? Explain why or why not. What detail in the story would help medieval people to believe it?

3.9 The Monastery

A reconstruction showing what Inch Abbey, Co. Down, would have looked like in 1300

As explained in Unit 2.1, Ireland had dozens of monasteries long before the Normans came, but these did not have elaborate buildings like those in France. The purpose of a monastery was to provide a secluded place where those who wanted a religious life could cut themselves off from the world and devote their time to prayer and the study of holy books. Men entered a **monastery** and women entered a **nunnery** (or convent).

Those entering the religious life took vows:

1. Vow of obedience — to obey the abbot or abbess in charge.
2. Vow of poverty — to give up all personal possessions.
3. Vow of chastity — to have no sexual relations.

Men entering a monastery had the tops of their heads shaved to show they were devoting themselves to God. Nuns wore a wimple covering the head and neck. There were many different orders of monks e.g. Benedictine, Carthusian and Dominican. Each had their own form of dress and their own rules.

The Cistercians

The most important religious order in Ireland was the Cistercian Order. They were founded in France in 1098, and were brought to Ireland by St. Malachy who founded Mellifont in 1142. They followed a reformed Benedictine rule, and believed in self-sufficiency. They grew all their own food and the lay brothers spent a lot of time farming. Cistercians kept sheep and even made their own habits out of sheep's wool. As their habits were wool-coloured they were called 'white monks'.

The Norman, John de Courcy, brought the Cistercians to Ulster. He founded Inch Abbey, near Downpatrick, in 1180, and his wife, Affreca, founded Grey Abbey, in the Ards Peninsula.

The artist's reconstruction at the top of this page shows Inch Abbey as it would have looked about 1300. Look back to page 53. What style of Gothic architecture has it?

The remains of Inch Abbey as they look today.

Although the size of each room varied, the layout of all Cistercian monasteries is the same. Study the diagram of Inch Abbey on this page. Note the large cruciform (cross-shaped) **church**, facing roughly east. On the south side is the **cloister** where the monks could relax or meditate. The eastern wing had the **vestry** (where vestments and service equipment were kept); the **chapter house** (where a chapter of the rules was read every day); the **parlour** (where conversation was allowed); and a long **day-room** (for indoor activities). Upstairs was the **dormitory** where the monks all slept. The monks ate in the **refectory** which was in the southern wing along with the **kitchen**.

Nearby, Inch had another two buildings, one of which was probably an **infirmary** (hospital) and the other a **bakehouse** for baking bread.

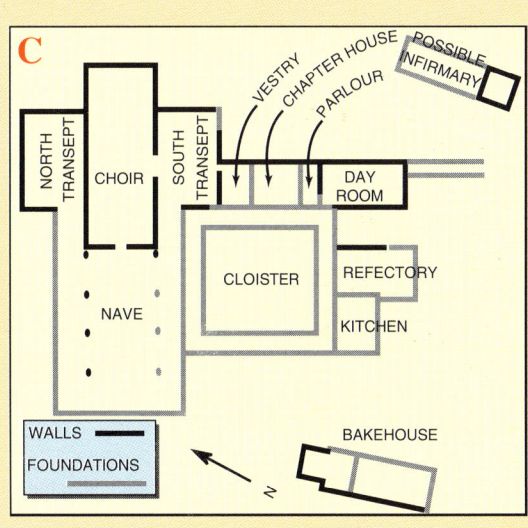

A diagram of Inch Abbey

Activities

1. Make a list of all the rooms in Inch Abbey. Try to find out as much as you can about what each one was used for.
2. Make an enlarged copy of the diagram above. Label each room clearly.

D

Holy Cross Abbey: the Abbey church and the east range. What was the upstairs used for? The three doors (left to right) led to (1) the Chapter House; (2) a passage which led to the Abbot's house; (3) the parlour.

Holy Cross Abbey

Holy Cross Abbey in Co. Tipperary is the best preserved Irish medieval monastery. Like Inch, it was a Cistercian Abbey founded in the 12th century, but it was largely rebuilt and modernised in the 15th century with decorated style windows and cloisters. For centuries the Abbey was a ruin. It was restored to its present state in the early 1970's. Using Holy Cross we can imagine life in a monastery very vividly.

Monks and nuns followed a very rigorous life in which their day was broken up by attendance at prayers. To make sure they did not fall asleep, the seats were hard and very narrow in the church. You can see seats like these in the cloisters at Holy Cross (Source E). Even so, they did not always listen attentively, as Source F shows.

A **pilgrimage** was a special journey to some holy place.

A **lay brother** was a servant in a monastery.

2.00 a.m.	Prayers (Matins).
3.00 a.m.	Back to bed.
6.00 a.m.	Prayers (Prime).
6.30 a.m.	Breakfast (bread and ale).
7.00 a.m.	Meeting in Chapter House. Monks who broke rules are disciplined. Tasks set for the day. Prayers.
8.00 a.m.	Lay brothers work in the fields or kitchen. Religious brothers walk in the cloisters, meditate or study.
11.00 a.m.	Prayers and communion.
Noon	Main meal, usually eaten in silence.
12.30 p.m.	Prayers.
1.00 p.m.	Lay brothers work in the fields. Religious brothers work in the gardens, fish, or relax.
6.00 p.m.	Prayers. (Vespers)
7.00 p.m.	Supper.
8.00 p.m.	Prayers (Compline). Retire to bed.

A typical day for a monk. Each service had its own Latin name.

Pilgrimages

The most exciting religious event in the Middle Ages was to go on a **pilgrimage** to some very holy place. Canterbury in England became an important place of pilgrimage because of the murder there of Archbishop Becket (St. Thomas). In Ireland the most famous pilgrimage was to Lough Derg, where St. Patrick's Island was supposed to be the entrance to Purgatory. Holy Cross in Co. Tipperary attracted pilgrims because it had a piece of wood believed to have come from the true cross.

Pilgrims were given free food and shelter at monasteries and enjoyed a sort of holiday. They went for various reasons — as a punishment for sins, to get a cure for the sick, or simply as an excuse to leave the village. Pilgrims collected small cap badges from shrines they had visited, to prove they had been.

F

We have convinced ourselves by clear proof that some nuns of your house bring with them to church birds, rabbits, hounds and such like things ... and give more thought to them than to the services of the church ... to the grievous peril of their souls.

Bishop of Winchester to the Abbess of Romsey, 1387.

The north cloister looking east. The wooden seats on the left were used by the monks to sit and meditate. What would the cloisters have been like in winter?

The cloisters. The green area to the centre was used for recreation such as bowls. The building on the left had cellars on the ground floor and a dormitory for the lay brothers.

?

1. How many times in the day did the monks attend prayers?
2. What might have attracted people to become monks or nuns (other than being very religious)?
3. Why do you think pilgrimages were regarded as so exciting?

3.10 1348: The Black Death

In 1348 a terrible plague called the **Black Death** reached England. It had been travelling across Europe from Asia along the world's trade routes. It was a killer, and medieval doctors had no idea what caused it. If you caught it you came out in black spots (Source A). Sores developed and then burst. You died in agony, usually within 5 days (Source B). Within three years it killed a third of the population of Europe. In 1349 it reached Ireland. If you caught the plague, you had only a 10% hope of surviving.

A

In men and women alike it first showed itself by the appearance of swellings in the groin or armpits. Some grew as large as an apple or an egg. From these two parts of the body this deadly swelling soon began to spread in all directions. Then black spots began to appear on the arms or thigh.

From the introduction to *The Decameron* by Boccaccio 1351

WHAT PEOPLE AT THE TIME THOUGHT CAUSED..

- Jews or nobles had poisoned the water
- Punishment from God
- Poison vapours from an earthquake in Jan 1348
- The close position of Saturn, Jupiter and Mars in 1345

THE BLACK DEATH

CURES

- Shut yourself away from everyone and drink only milk or wine
- Flog yourself to show you are sorry for your sins (Sources D & F)
- Leave the towns and flee to the countryside
- Cover your mouth with a mask or carry herbs
- Carry on as normal and hope for the best

B

This pestilence was so contagious that those who touched the dead or persons sick with the plague were straightaway infected themselves and died. Many died from boils and ulcers and running sores which grew on the legs and beneath the armpits while others suffered pains in the head and went almost into a frenzy, whilst others spat blood.

Written by a Franciscan monk, Kilkenny, Ireland.

C

Take a live frog and lay the belly of it next to the plague sore; if the patient will escape, the frog will burst in a quarter of an hour; then lay on another; and this you do till no more burst, for they draw forth the poison. If none of the frogs do burst, the person will not escape.

Contemporary cure for the plague

D

Flagellants beating each other at Doornik in 1349. From *The Chronicle of Aegidus Li Muisis* (14th century).

F

They gathered together in large groups and marched in procession with their backs bare. When they got to crossroads, or to the market squares of towns, they formed circles and beat their bare backs with weighted whips ... The flagellants lashed at their shoulders and arms with whips which had iron points at the end. They whipped themselves so hard they drew blood...

Description of the Flagellants by Jean de Venette, 14th century

E

A grave slab in Drogheda made at the time of the Black Death in Ireland.

What caused it?

The Plague was probably a mixture of **bubonic plague** which caused the swellings (buboes) and **pneumonic plague** which still affects parts of Asia. The germ which caused it was identified in 1894. It is carried by fleas which live on black rats. If the flea bit a human, the human caught the Plague. Some modern scientists think a lot of the deaths blamed on the Black Death were possibly caused by **anthrax** or even **smallpox**.

The effects of the Black Death

1. The population of England fell from 5 million to 2.5 million. It did not reach 5 million again until 1650.
2. A strange group of monks, called Flagellants, appeared. (Sources D and F)
3. Medieval people became very obsessed with death. (Source E)
4. Peasants died and complete villages were abandoned.
5. The Lords of the Manor found there was a shortage of peasants to work their land.
6. Peasants realised this and demanded higher wages. Wages rose by up to 50%.

?

1. Using Sources A and B list all the symptoms of the Black Death. Try to avoid listing the same symptom twice.

2. How was the cure in Source C supposed to work? Do you think it would work?

3. Study the section "What caused it?" If this had been known in 1348, how could people have reduced their chances of catching the Black death?

4. Using the information and sources in this unit, do you think the poor were any more likely to catch the Plague than the rich?

3.11 1381 The Peasants' Revolt

In 1377 **Richard II** became king at the age of 10. He introduced the Poll Tax. In 1380 the Poll Tax was trebled. Many peasants avoided paying by hiding or telling lies about the number in their family. In March 1381 King Richard ordered the arrest of anyone who refused to pay the Poll Tax. **John Ball** was one of those imprisoned. The **Peasants' Revolt** which followed was the most serious event of its kind in the Middle Ages.

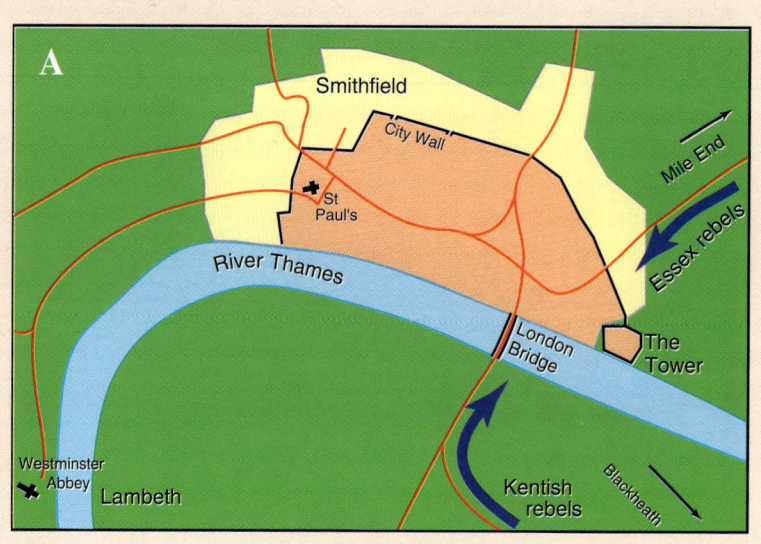

London in 1381

Causes

1 WAGES: There was discontent among the peasants because Parliament in 1351 had passed the **Statute of Labourers**. This stopped them from being paid higher wages than they got in 1347 (before the Black Death).

2 AGITATION: Preachers such as John Ball, a priest in Kent, and peasant leaders like Wat Tyler stirred up the people by saying that all men should be equal and that the poor should not pay taxes.

3 TAXES: To pay for a war in France, the government in 1377 taxed peasants as well as the nobility for the first time. They invented the Poll Tax. 'Poll' means 'head'. Everyone over 15 had to pay. In 1377 they paid 4d (old pennies), in 1379 4d, and in 1380, 12d.

Time line of the Revolt

May
Commissioners are sent by the king to find the tax dodgers. Riots break out in Essex and Kent. Some tax collectors are murdered.

June 6
Kentish peasants capture Rochester Castle. They march to Maidstone and release John Ball. **Wat Tyler** chosen as leader.

June 10
Led by Wat Tyler, peasants go to Canterbury and destroy the palace of **Simon Sudbury**, Archbishop of Canterbury. Sudbury had introduced the Poll Tax.

June 11
Peasants from Essex and Kent march to London.

June 12
The Essex rebels camp at Mile End, near London. The Kentish rebels camp at Blackheath. Richard II and the government take refuge in the Tower of London.

June 13
John Ball preaches to the rebels at Blackheath. (Source B) The King tries to speak to them from a boat on the Thames, then returns to the Tower. The rebels enter London and behead several royal officials. Palaces are burnt.

June 14
Richard II, the Mayor and some lords meet the rebels at Mile End. Wat Tyler states his demands:
- freedom for all men
- abolition of all labour service to lords
- fair wages for everyone
- no more Poll Taxes

- 60 -

B

Picture painted about 1460 showing the events of June 15. On the left, Wat Tyler is attacked and on the right Richard II faces the peasants.

C

Good people, all is not well in England, nor will they be until everyone is equal and there are neither villeins nor gentlemen, and Lords are no greater than we are ... They are dressed in velvet, while we have to wear poor cloth. They have wines, spices and fine bread, while we have to make do with coarse bread and water. They have fine houses while we have to work in the wind and rain of the fields. Let us go to the King, he is young, and show him what slavery we are in. Let us tell him that we want things to be put right or else we will do something about it ourselves.

From John Ball's sermon at Blackheath, quoted by Jean Froissart, *Chronicle*, about 1390.

- a free pardon for everyone who had come to London
- punishment for the King's 'evil advisers'.

While the King is at Mile End, Kent rebels enter the Tower and execute 4 advisers, including Sudbury. Riots in London.

June 15

The King, with 200 followers, meets the rebels at Smithfield. Tyler makes more demands and speaks rudely to the King. He is attacked and mortally wounded. The peasants draw their bows and are about to shoot when Richard II says "Sirs, will ye shoot your King? I will be your Captain. Follow me". He leads them out of London. His officials behead Tyler. The King gives out charters agreeing to Tyler's demands and the peasants go home contented.

Results of the Revolt

A week later the King went back on his promises. He arrested all the rebel leaders and executed them. The charters were torn up. The King said "Peasants you are and peasants you will remain". A wave of terror followed in the villages of Kent and Essex.

The revolt really frightened the government. The King never again tried to collect the Poll Tax. Parliament still tried to keep down wages, but after a few years it gave up. Gradually over the next 100 years the system of labour service was abandoned.

?

1. What would the following have thought of John Ball's sermon — (a) the peasants who heard him (b) the lords in London (c) King Richard II ?

2. What part was played in the Peasants' Revolt by (a) John Ball (b) Wat Tyler (c) the King.

3. Why do you think the revolt failed? Try to pick out the event which was the turning point for the rebels.

4. What results of the rebellion were (a) good and (b) bad for the peasants?

5. What features of Source B are the artist's imagination?

3.12　　　　The Norman Legacy

Norman surname still in evidence in Carlingford, Co. Louth

During the period covered by this book, life had changed a great deal for people in England, Scotland, Wales and Ireland. Many new things had been invented e.g. the spinning wheel, guns and gunpowder. The first **windmills** had appeared about the time of the Battle of Hastings. Between 1350 and 1390 the first **public clocks** appeared in churches. In 1477 **William Caxton** started the first **printing press** in England. European explorers had sailed by sea to Africa, India and China. In 1492 **Columbus discovered America**. Much more was known about the world than was known in 1066.

Today we can still see a lot of things which have survived from the Middle Ages, and which are part of the legacy which has been left to us by the Normans. Here are some of the permanent effects which the Normans and their successors have left here in Ireland:

Language. The official language of the Irish Republic is Irish, a language which is loved by many people. But most people in Ireland, north and south, use English as their everyday language. English was brought to Ireland by the Normans and has remained ever since.

Castles. All over Ireland there are castles, some still lived in and used, but most ruined. There are over 2000 castles in Ireland and most of them were built in the Middle Ages. In many parts of Ulster, like Clough, Co. Down, we can see the remains of the Norman motte and bailey castles.

Law and Government. The Normans and their successors began to replace the ancient system of Irish law with English Common Law. Our laws today are based on this law. The Normans were the first to introduce parliaments to Ireland, and the first to begin to divide Ireland into counties.

Churches. The modern Roman Catholic Church in Ireland is very much the legacy of the changes to the organisation of the church introduced by the Normans in the Middle Ages. A more visible sign of the Normans is the ruins of monasteries and abbeys visible in many parts of Ireland.

Towns. Before the Normans there were no towns in Ireland apart from the Viking settlements like Dublin. Many towns founded by the Normans — Carrickfergus, Ardglass, Carlingford — still exist today.

Surnames. Many of the family names of Ireland today have Norman origins. A number of names begin with 'Fitz'. This means 'son of'. Fitzstephen means 'son of Stephen'. Here are some Norman names still common today: Burke, Butler, Costello, Fitzgerald, Fitzmaurice, Power, Roche, Savage, Walsh (Source A).

Norman and Plantagenet Kings

Chronology

Norman

1066-1087	William I
1087-1100	William II
1100-1135	Henry I
1135-1154	Stephen

Plantagenet

1154-1189	Henry II
1189-1199	Richard I
1199-1216	John
1216-1272	Henry III
1272-1307	Edward I
1307-1327	Edward II
1327-1377	Edward III
1377-1399	Richard II
1399-1413	Henry IV
1413-1422	Henry V
1422-1461	Henry VI
1461-1483	Edward IV
1483	Edward V
1483-1485	Richard III

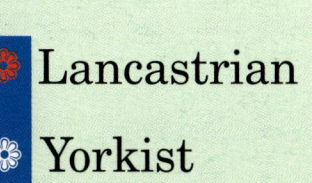

❀ Lancastrian
✸ Yorkist

1042	Edward the Confessor king
1066	Halley's Comet
	Reign of Harold
	Battle of Hastings
	Harrying of the North
1086	Domesday Book
1166	Exile of Dermot MacMurrough
1169	Normans arrive in Ireland
1170	Murder of Archbishop Becket
1175	Treaty of Windsor
1190-3	Third Crusade
1215	Magna Carta
1224	First Franciscan Friary
1301	Edward II made first Prince of Wales
1314	Battle of Bannockburn (Scotland)
1346	Battle of Crécy (France)
1348	Black Death
1351	Statute of Labourers
1381	Peasants' Revolt
1415	Battle of Agincourt (France)
1431	Death of Joan of Arc
1453	End of Hundred Years' War
1455	Start of Wars of the Roses
1461	Henry VI deposed
1470	Edward VI expelled
	Henry VI reinstated
1471	Henry VI killed at Battle of Tewkesbury
1485	Battle of Bosworth (England)
	Henry Tudor becomes Henry VII

Index

Architecture	52 - 53	Inch Abbey	54 - 55
Ardglass	39	Ireland	7, 20 - 31, 33
Armagh	49, 53	Isle of Man	25, 30, 38

Ball, John	60 - 61	Lacy, Hugh de	26, 27, 31
Bannockburn	33	Law and Order	51
Bayeux Tapestry	4, 9, 10, 13, 14, 18 - 19, 44, 46	Llywelyn the Great	32
Becket, Thomas	26, 27, 57		
Black Death	58 - 59	MacMurrough, Dermot	20 -25, 26
Bruce, Robert	33	Mellifont	21, 22, 54
		Monasteries	20, 21, 53, 54 - 57
		Monks	8, 21, 54 - 57
Canute, King	8, 10		
Carlingford	48, 49, 62		
Carrickfergus	30, 38, 40, 41, 43, 49	Odo	11, 19
Cashel	21, 27	O'Connor, Rory	20, 23, 24, 27
Castles	17, 36 - 41, 43		
Church, The	35, 52 - 57		
Cistercians	22, 54 - 56	Pilgrimages	57
Clough	36		
Courcy, John de	27, 28 - 31		
		Richard II	60 - 61
Downpatrick	29, 30, 49, 54		
		Salisbury	50, 52
		Scotland	7, 25, 33
Edgar, Prince	10, 16	Stamford Bridge	11
Edward I	32, 33	Strongbow	24 - 27
Edward the Confessor	8, 9, 10		
		Tralee	48, 49, 50, 51
Feudalism	34 - 35	Tyler, Wat	60 - 61
Flagellants	59		
		Ulster History Park	21, 37, 46
Guilds	51		
		Wales	7, 23, 24, 26, 32
		William I (see William, Duke of Normandy)	
Harald Hardrada	10, 11, 13		
Harold II, King of England	8 - 15	William, Duke of Normandy	6, 9 - 13, 16 - 19
Hastings	12 - 15, 16, 18, 19	Windsor, Treaty of	27, 29
Henry II	22, 23, 26, 27, 28, 31		
Hereward the Wake	17		
Holy Cross Abbey	53, 56 - 57		